Paper *Kisses*

Bond Book

This book is one of 155,000 in a special purchase to upgrade the CALS collection. Funds for the project were approved by Little Rock voters on 8/17/04.

✓

REINHARD KAISER

Paper Kisses

A TRUE LOVE STORY

TRANSLATED BY ANTHEA BELL

Other Press · New York

Originally published as Königskinder by Reinhard Kaiser.
Copyright © Schöffling & Co. Verlagsbuchhandlung GmbH, Frankfurt am
Main 1996

The publication of this work was supported by a grant from the Goethe-Institut.

Translation copyright © 2006 Anthea Bell

ISBN-13: 978-1-59051-181-7

Production Editor: Robert D. Hack
Text designed and set by Natalya Balnova

10 9 8 7 6 5 4 3 2 1

Library of Congress Cataloging-in-Publication Data

Kaiser, Reinhard.
  [Königskinder. English]
  Paper kisses : a true love story / by Reinhard Kaiser ; translated from
the German by Anthea Bell.
    p. cm.
  ISBN 1-59051-181-6 (pbk. : alk. paper) 1. Kaufmann, Rudolf, 1909-1946.
2. Jews—Germany—Biography. 3. Geologists—Germany—Biography. 4. Magnusson,
Ingeborg, d. 1972. 5. Germany—History—1933-1945. 6. Germany—Ethnic relations.
I. Title.
  DS135.G5K38513 2006
  940.53'18'092—dc22

                                                        2005019364

Paper Kisses

I WAS NOT LOOKING for stories when I found Rudolf Kaufmann's first letters to Ingeborg Magnusson—in May 1991, at a stamp auction in Frankfurt. There were over seven thousand lots on offer, and before the auction I asked to see ten or a dozen of them, lots that I had marked in the sale catalogue. It described Lot 6673 as: "Germany, c. 1890-1955, large collection of stamps (unused, in mint condition, or postmarked), including bundled items, also cards, letters, and parcel despatch notes from the German Reich, etc., varying condition, extremely high catalogue value! Reserve, DM 500.00."

On viewing, the lot turned out to be a carton containing albums, card mounts, semiopaque cellophane bags, and cigar boxes full of stamps. Among all the run-of-the-mill stuff and a few philatelic curiosities, I came upon a batch of some thirty envelopes, all sent by the same person between 1935 and 1939 from Königsberg and other German cities, all hand-addressed to the same woman at the same address in Stockholm. The envelopes still had letters inside them.

Viewing at an auction doesn't give you time to read anything thoroughly. However, even a brief glance at two or three of these letters showed that they dealt, at some length, with a love affair of the period just before the Second World War. That was all I knew when I decided to bid for the carton and its entire contents: stamps, history, and the stories it contained.

When it came to the auction, there proved to be considerable interest in Lot 6673. What stamp auctioneers describe in their reports as a battle of the bids broke out. I wouldn't have gone above twice the reserve for the stamps alone, but my curiosity to know what was in those letters kept me bidding even beyond three times that amount. The longer I went on raising the card with my bidding number on it, however, the less I could see why anyone without my double motive—because I wanted the stamps *and* the story—would force the price for the lot up so high. In the end I was bidding against a single determined opponent, a man I couldn't see. The auction room was L-shaped. I was sitting in the long arm of the L and my adversary in its short arm, while the auctioneer stood at his desk in the angle between them, turning to me and the other bidder in turn, reciting his counting-out rhyme as the figures moved in monotonous but unnerving leaps of fifty at a time toward two thousand Deutschmarks.

Stamps have their market price. Some may be rare, but very, very few are unique. Fantasy prices are hardly ever paid for stamps. Yet a man bidding anything at all, high or low, for a story he doesn't yet know is paying a fantasy price anyway. That was what I was doing on that Saturday afternoon in May 1991.

I took the carton I had bought home, eager to find out what it contained, but unprepared for a story that would not loosen its hold on me for years.

Mine lilla kaere Ingeborg, my dear little Ingeborg, you won't have forgotten me and your visit to Bologna in spite of the beauties of Venice.

Those two lovely days still make me feel wonderful. The only trouble is they were too short. All I have left are the photographs of you smiling at me "like a girl in love." If you want any of the pictures, write and tell me and I'll make you enlargements. There's Sheet I and Sheet II, and the numbering goes like this:

1 2 3

4 5 6

7 8 9

10 11 12

For instance, Sheet I, no. 8. I'm already looking forward to hearing from you. I hope you're really enjoying Venice. Your red nose came out beautifully, of course! I'm going to S. Luca on Sunday, and I'll think of you. Write soon and tell me when you'll be passing through Greifswald. I'll let my friends know. I mean, say when you're leaving Berlin. I send you a very, very loving kiss. Your Rudolf.

An undated card, no bigger than a playing card, both sides covered with small handwriting in black ink, and sending a kiss—perhaps the first kiss he sends her by letter because he can't give it in person. The real kisses exchanged in Bologna, the kisses preceding this paper kiss, are all gone now. The memory of such real kisses lingers on while the lovers who once gave them are still alive, and after that I suppose nothing is left. However, the paper kiss sent right across Europe by mail sixty years ago has been preserved. There it is for anyone to read, once a contact between the two of them, bridging space, now a contact between them and us, bridging time.

They met in Bologna early in the summer of 1935—a young German from Königsberg and a Swedish girl from Stockholm. Ingeborg Magnusson was on vacation in Italy, visiting Florence,

Rome, and Bologna. Rudolf Kaufmann had been in Bologna for several months, but not because he wanted to see the country

and its people, not of his own free will. It was the situation in Germany that had sent him to Italy. Which was lucky for him, as it turned out, for if he had not been in Bologna in the summer of 1935 he would never have met Ingeborg Magnusson.

The ground had begun to crumble beneath his feet some time before. He had been living in a vacuum for two years, and had always found it hard to cope with it. Now he suddenly didn't mind. Now he felt he was floating, even flying—with her, beside her, for a day in Bologna, for a second day in Venice, when he followed her there. Then their time ran out. Their ways parted. Inge went back to Stockholm, he returned to Bologna. They began corresponding. Her letters to him have not been preserved; his letters to her survive. The small, undated card seems to have been the first.

Early in that summer of 1935, in Bologna, Rudolf Kaufmann was expecting visitors from Germany. His elder brother Hans and Hans's wife Vera, on vacation in Italy, had said they would come to see him. With them, an unexpected but immediately welcome guest, came their "delightful traveling companion," a young woman from Sweden.

Just how Rudolf Kaufmann and Ingeborg Magnusson came closer to each other in the brief time they had available is not quite clear from the hints in the letters. But anyway, photographs were involved.

As soon as he had seen her for the first time, he sent a photograph of himself to her at the hotel where she was staying—a bold, even impertinent move, but she did not think it intrusive. Indeed, she was delighted, and had already kissed the picture many times before exchanging a first kiss with its subject.

For his part, he seems to have been smitten while looking at her through the lens of the "multiplicator camera" that he used in the Multifoto studio where he worked in Bologna. Perhaps he fell in love with her as he captured her picture on photographic plates—there SHE was, thirty times over: thirty pictures of her. Twelve small stamp-sized photographs fitted on a single plate in rows of three and columns of four. Thirty pictures on two and a half plates. Perhaps he didn't ask her to "say cheese" from where he stood behind the camera. Perhaps he plucked up his courage and suggested, instead, "Why don't you just smile at me *like a girl in love?*"

Or perhaps it wasn't like that at all.

However, they certainly went together to San Luca, outside Bologna and situated on a hill with fine views. You reached it by cable car. The letters are quite clear about that. They often return to the subject of San Luca: the air there, the grass, the wine and the fettucine, the tough roast meat, the mountain, the flowers, the rocks, and the glowworms. In his letters, Rudolf Kaufmann calls the cable car a *suspension railway*.

Rudolf Kaufmann

Perhaps Inge was traveling with Hans and Vera in a large group that had to follow a set itinerary, so she could not simply stay on in Bologna, as she might have wished. When she went to Venice, Rudolf Kaufmann was left behind in Bologna at first, undecided. He already guessed how much he would miss her, but only when the people who sublet him a room in Bologna told him that she had phoned while he was out, asking for him, did he catch the

Ingeborg Magnusson

next train to the city by the sea, in such haste that he forgot to take his shaving things, so that when they met his stubble scratched her face with all their kissing. Venice was a wonderful experience. They went for a ride in a gondola and looked around St. Mark's. They climbed a tower in which no one else took any interest. Inge screamed when he suddenly turned *so wild* in the dim light, and he silenced her with his scratchy kisses, one on each landing of the stairway. By the time they reached the top she looked like a shaggy poodle.

That summer of 1935, Rudolf Kaufmann had his first stroke of luck in a long time—a piece of good luck amidst all the bad.

Two years earlier, he had had another singular stroke of luck. He had been dismissed from his post at Greifswald University because he was Jewish. Instability had already set in. However, his doctoral thesis had been published in the proceedings of the Greifswald Geological and Paleontological Institute just in the nick of time, early in 1933. It was dated 1 February, two days after Germany had acclaimed a new Reich Chancellor who immediately, in a radio broadcast, asked the German people to give him, their new Chancellor, four years. Rudolf Kaufmann had never taken any special interest in politics. His thesis was on the evolutionary history of a class of marine fossil arthropods known as trilobites. It took the trilobites two hundred and fifty million years or more to come to anything.

Tomorrow I'm sending you all the geological material I've written. I can hardly believe I did all those studies. I'm very proud of my great work on the trilobites, because I was the first person to prove there's a continuous, purposeful line of development in the history of those creatures. I expect to be far better known years hence than I am now, once the zoologists and paleontologists begin to understand my work properly. I'm enclosing another photograph of myself. You might like it.

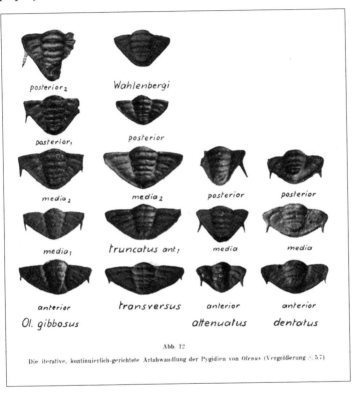

Abb. 12

Die iterative, kontinuierlich-gerichtete Artabwandlung der Pygidien von *Olenus* (Vergrößerung ×, 5.7)

Trilobite specimens from Rudolf Kaufmann's thesis

Rudolf Kaufmann's doctoral thesis must have made it easier for him to find posts outside Germany, and for a while he was still able to continue working in his own field. He spent a few months in Copenhagen in 1934, then went to the Geological Institute in Bologna, again on a temporary basis, and on terms that meant he had to earn himself a living—in the Multifoto studio.

Kaufmann finds the heat in Italy harder to bear once Inge has left for Stockholm and he is back in Bologna. Even before meeting her, he has toyed with the idea of returning to Germany. Now he has another good reason to go back, and it is the deciding factor: Germany, and more particularly East Prussia, is closer than Italy to Sweden. Kaufmann is impatiently waiting for his brother to send news from Königsberg. Hans has promised to put out feelers for any opportunities, any prospect of a post that would give him a new start. There are grounds for hope. After two years in power, the new political masters are firmly ensconced. By now they themselves must be feeling distaste for the petty fanaticism that helped them in their struggle and their rise to power. The frenzy will die down. It must die down. Perhaps it has died down already.

All the same, doubts mingle with Kaufmann's confidence as he plans his return. The new courage he has felt since his two days with Inge is beset by misgivings. He doesn't know what really awaits him in Germany, and she herself has far less an idea of what she will really be letting herself in for if she pledges herself to him. Ought he hope that she will?

You would be just the right lifelong companion for me. But I have to keep reminding myself that I have no right to love anyone. It's so hard to know where life will take me. I've been in limbo for two years now and I'm no further on. When will I ever be able to look after myself and someone else, the one I love? I don't know if I'll be any better off in Königsberg. Even my brother doesn't feel perfectly secure in his job. He could be dismissed any time because of his origins.

Half in earnest, half knowing that she is unlikely to heed such scruples, he advises her to give him up. Suppose another man, some Per or Jens or Ulle, turns up one day offering her a home, why then, he says, she mustn't spare a thought for him, Rudolf—at least, not until he has *a firmer footing in life.* And as a corrective to the love story beginning to develop between them he quotes two other stories, two love stories with unhappy endings from which the protagonists have only half recovered—their own earlier love affairs, hers and his. In Bologna, Inge told him how she once waited a long time for a man she loved who lived far away, and how badly she was let down in the end. He reminds her of that now, and mentions his girlfriend Hanni; he was happy with Hanni for over a year in Greifswald.

We were even officially engaged. Then, two years ago, came the great change in Germany, and her father said I wasn't to have anything more to do with her. But she said she'd always stand by me. However, she hasn't written for over six months now, not that she wrote much before, and I've heard she's going to marry someone else in the autumn. But I know she's still fond of me. And I was completely faithful to her, too, until I suddenly met this blonde poodle from Sweden.

At twenty-eight, Ingeborg Magnusson is two years older than Rudolf Kaufmann. She works for an insurance company in Stockholm; she would rather have gone into advertising or become an interpreter, but during the Depression jobs weren't easy to find anywhere, Sweden included. She could consider herself lucky to have a job at all. She writes and speaks fluent German, and she knows Italian and English, too. She sends Rudolf Kaufmann a packet of books in Bologna, and he immediately resolves to improve his Swedish; he already has a basic grasp of the language. He has been to Sweden on several occasions over the last few years, and indeed has spent some time there excavating and researching. The trilobites whose evolution was the subject of his doctoral thesis come from an alum quarry in the Skåne region, where he single-handedly collected, measured, and compared them. If he is ever to be with Inge he wants to speak only Swedish to her, he says. Until then, they write their letters mainly in German.

Now and then Rudolf Kaufmann inserts a few Italian words into his letters—private remarks, not meant to be understood by everyone who might set eyes on them. Sweet-sounding terms of affection in the language of the country where they met, or comments that he scribbled quickly on the back of the envelope after sealing it: *Chiusa con baci,* "closed with kisses"; and another time, on a rather crumpled envelope: *Ti ho troppo abbraciato, per questo è cosi maltratta questa lettera!* "I have embraced you too much, which is why this letter is so mistreated."

The German authorities don't understand Italian embraces. They don't believe those extravagant protestations of true love; they get suspicious. They take the crumpling for an indication that banknotes have been enclosed, which is against the law, and mistreat the letter yet further. They slit it open and look to see what's in it. They do this blatantly, not in secret. Finding nothing, they seal the envelope again with a tape on which the words "Opened by Customs for reasons of currency regulations" appear four times and are impossible to overlook. Inge is worried. She asks her lover to be more cautious, but he himself doesn't care about unauthorized readers.

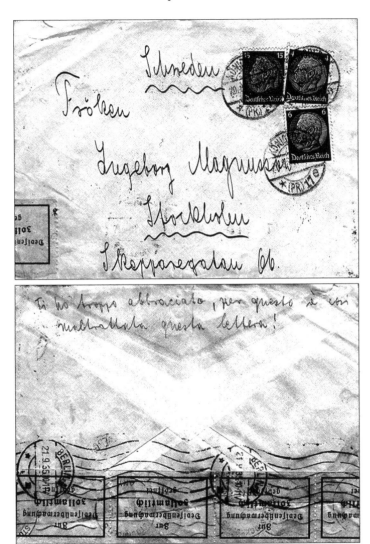

It doesn't matter if they keep opening my letters. Anyone's welcome to
know that we're in love and how we long for each other. Still, I won't
write any more Italian on the back of the envelope.

During their time together in Bologna they were already making plans to meet again, and the letters they write each other after that are full of projects for further meetings. The question is very simple: either he comes to her or she goes to him. Or they meet somewhere in the middle. Rudolf Kaufmann is familiar with Stockholm and its surroundings, and knows that it will all be even better with Inge. The island of Gotland, roughly halfway between her and him, is well placed, too. And if she comes to see him in Königsberg:

then my brother must lend us the collapsible boat and the tent, and we'll go to the Kurische Nehrung in Lithuania, where there's nothing but dunes, woods, and water, no human beings. We'll put our tent up, stay there cooking and walking and bathing together, and we won't bother about anyone because there'll be no one else there.

So he imagines it.

At the end of July 1935 Rudolf Kaufmann returns to Germany, traveling by way of Königsberg to the Samland peninsula on the Baltic to see his father, who has a summer holiday house in Georgenswalde.

It's a seaside resort on our beautiful coast. The weather's stormy at the moment, and when it's like that I gaze far, far into the distance, far to the northwest, because I know that a dear, good girl is standing by the same waters over there, gazing back at me and wanting to be all mine. Oh, Ingelein, little Inge, how stupid life is. It's being made so difficult for me here. Two months ago, when Hans suggested that I should come back to Germany and start a training in the grain trade, it seemed a good idea. But everything has changed so much since then. You'll have read about it. When I went to see my old professor at Greifswald, he didn't even dare invite me to the Institute. Other people could have used that against him. And I'm afraid to

*visit my old friends here too, in case I make things difficult for them.
For the same reason I'm not likely to be taken on as a trainee in any
local business. I would never have thought that people would act so
harshly here. I wouldn't be able to set up as a photographer either.
Inge, my dearest little poodle child, I've been reproaching myself for
giving you that kiss on S. Luca, and many others after it. But I'm so
glad and happy about them all the same.*

After the contretemps with his professor at Greifswald, the
same thing happens to Kaufmann when he comes back to
Königsberg, and meets two old friends for the first time in ages.
Benno and Wolfgang are still very nice people, he tells Inge in
a letter.

*But I realize that my company would only make things difficult for
them. There's so much gossip about, you've no idea.*

So he plans to live very quietly in Königsberg, seeing only a few
people. He's almost used to that by now, and will make up for it
by spending more time in his thoughts with Inge in Stockholm.
At least the lonely struggle that costs him so much is over now.
He's not alone any more.

*After 2 long, bitter years, when I met you in Italy you were the sunny
day I'd been yearning for so long.*

To dispel gloomy thoughts he takes up athletics again, joins a
newly founded Jewish sports club, and acts as a trainer. Besides
studying geology, he has taken an examination qualifying
him to teach gymnastics. The regular exercise does him

good, he writes.

*However, I don't intend to tell you about everything here. . . . I just
don't want to write about all these things, and you mustn't either.
Please don't. Or someone else could snap all this up.*

But it is not only, and not primarily, the fear of gossip and a
stranger's eyes seeing the letters that keeps him from writing
about *everything here*. He isn't going to complain, because com-
plaints can sound pathetic at a distance. He doesn't want her
pity, doesn't want to figure as a helpless victim of overwhelming
circumstances. He wants to be the *wild man* she loves, so he
conceals his dismay at the situation in Germany as best he can.
He hopes to invite her to see him as soon as possible, and when
she comes he wants her to feel at ease, as if she were floating on
air with him, beside him. So he doesn't like to describe
Germany in gloomy colors. But as he cannot paint a bright picture of it (apart from those few places where there are no other
human beings, and where he goes with her in his dreams), he
prefers to paint no picture at all. Over long periods, he leaves
out mention of *all these things*, instead sending her large numbers of written kisses. He writes about his love, his happiness at
having found her, the life they will lead together some day, the
life that in a way they have already begun to lead. On paper.

*I feel as if you were sitting here with me, and I were telling you all the
things that I'm really only writing down. And you fill my little room
with your love, and we're looking out at the big Schlossteich*—I live
close to it—and the full moon is shining into the room. We sit perfect-*

---

* *Literally, "castle pond": an ornamental lake in Königsberg.*

ly still, looking at each other with our souls in our eyes and enjoying the feeling that we belong together. And tomorrow you'll go shopping with me, because we really must get around to finding me a good hat. I hardly know myself how I'd look in a hat. All I have at the moment is a very light summer hat from Italy. But it's the fall now, and I need something less lightweight to wear on my head.

Is it mere chance that Rudolf Kaufmann becomes conscious of the approaching cold weather and his exposed, hatless situation on 16 September 1935? That is the day when a new law comes into force in Germany. Its first paragraph forbids marriage "between Jews and citizens of German or racially related blood," its second paragraph forbids sexual intercourse between them outside marriage, and finally, its fifth paragraph threatens those who infringe the law with prison and the penitentiary. Kaufmann will have read about this law in the newspaper. He does not mention it in his letters, either on this or on any other day. Instead he writes cheerfully about the hat he plans to buy with Inge's assistance. It is possible that his heart feels rather lighter now that he knows the exact wording of the new law. Up until now, uncertainty has reigned. The new law makes everything clear. Its provisions do not apply to him and Inge. He is indeed Jewish—according to those provisions—and if the blood that flows in Inge's veins is not German it is certainly "racially related." But luckily for both of them she is not a German citizen; she is Swedish. It is also possible that Rudolf Kaufmann has greeted the promulgation of the "Law for the Protection of German Blood and German Honor" with a kind of relief. Once again, he has been lucky in the circumstances.

Ever since Rudolf Kaufmann returned to Königsberg from the
Baltic coast he has been thinking about ways and means. His
major concern is to meet Inge again. He has many other widely
varying projects for finding a job and making a living. Every let-

ter to Stockholm describes new and large-scale plans, plans that cross national frontiers, and their success seems hardly to depend on himself at all—they are just vague hopes that scarcely even deserve that name, for most of them, if fulfilled, would take him even further from Inge and Stockholm than he was in Italy and Bologna.

30 July 1935: 2 weeks ago I was asked if I'd like to go to South America (Colombia) as a geologist or hydrologist. I've applied for the job. Unfortunately, I have to seize every opportunity I get to earn a living. But whether they'll take me on is very doubtful. I suddenly see so few prospects in Germany at the moment.

8 August: My prospects for the future aren't much better. I've put a general advertisement in a Berlin and Frankfurt newspaper. Perhaps someone will answer it.

18 August: At the moment I'm helping out for a grain-dealer's agent, a friend of Hans, whose clerk is getting married. . . . Well, I'm learning to be a businessman!* But the stupid thing is that I don't really feel cut out for the job. And no one knows how all this about not trading with non-Aryans will turn out. My brother has advised me to join the Zionists, which would mean taking a two-year agricultural training here and then going to Palestine as a laborer to settle there. Well, I suppose I'll have to, I can't see any alternative. But I'm afraid of the prospect, because I'd be living in circles quite unlike those I know.

28 August: I'm making every effort to see if I can't get some post as a geologist after all. At the moment, through the good offices of a gen-

---

* The literal meaning of Rudolf's surname Kaufmann.

tleman here, I've written a letter to a gold-prospecting company in Persia. *We poor creatures mustn't give up hope.*

16 September: I read about a group planning to emigrate to South America, people in my own situation going to Ecuador. I'll write to them. Perhaps they could do with a geologist there. If only there were any chance of work for me in Sweden.

That would indeed have been a piece of great good fortune. Kaufmann writes to Sven Hedin, the Swedish explorer of Asia, and gets an answer. But kind words are no concrete help. He writes to a professor at the Stockholm Riksmuseet, a man he had met in Sweden years ago. But his hopes of a secure life in Scandinavia is shattered. Academic posts are few and far between, Professor Stensiö writes back, and funds are limited. Sweden is the same as everywhere else in this respect. It isn't easy even to get there by sea. Since Kaufmann has been back in Königsberg, he has seen himself and Inge as the two royal children in Heine's poem, although they are better off than the prince and princess in the lyric.

We poor stupid creatures—here's one of us in Stockholm and the other in Königsberg. And we'd both like to be with each other. "There were two royal children, who loved one another dearly. They could not come together, so deep flowed the water, so clearly."* That's what the poem says. But today, with all our modern means of transport, it really ought to be possible for the two of us to meet. I'm going to look around and see if we can't at least meet one September Sunday in Gotland. It must be feasible somehow.

---

* *Es waren zwei Königskinder, die hatten einander so lieb. Sie konnten zusammen nicht kommen, das Wasser war viel zu tief.*

Gotland was well placed. Inge could come a good part of the way to meet him there. But travel by sea depends on the weather. There can be storms in the Baltic even in summer. Even in summer, ships have engine trouble. Shipping lines change the timetables of their steamers overnight. And it's not certain that if Kaufmann tries going to Gotland on a German freighter he won't encounter problems *because of his person*. Moreover, there are strict restrictions on taking currency out of the country for all Germans, not just Jews.

I hope it will be all right about the visa and the money. I'm not allowed to take more than 10 marks with me. You'll probably have to lend your man something once he's there. And then I must send it back to you in monthly installments of 10 marks at a time, with a large extra surcharge of kisses.

Early in October he finds a ship that, if all goes well, will set off for Stockholm in a few days' time. Also early in October, he mentions two offers that he has received as a result of his newspaper advertisement:

. . . one as private assistant to a scientist in Berlin. The other as gymnastics teacher in a school in Coburg, the "Preacher Hirsch Boarding School." For that second job, however, I'd probably need to be Jewish by religion too, which I'm not at the moment.

Although Rudolf Kaufmann's roots are Jewish, his religion, like his family's, is Evangelical Christianity. But it soon turns out that he can take the post as teacher at a Jewish school all the same.

My dear little signora, *hurrah, hurrah, the outcome of my newspaper ad is that I'm engaged by telegram for the job as teacher (gymnastics, etc.) at a Jewish boarding school in Coburg, Thuringia, starting on 15 October! It's 12 midnight, Saturday, I went straight to the post office to telegraph the school back and now I'm writing you a letter. I'm really supposed to start there on 1 October, but when I sent in my job application the day before yesterday I said it must be 15 October, because of you. Oh, how happy we'll be, all the happier now that I have prospects for the future. It was probably meant to happen like this. I took my gymnastic teacher's exam five years ago just for fun. I'd never have guessed how useful it would turn out. Yesterday evening they said the ship was leaving on Saturday evening. Now it's not till Monday. Who knows when it will really set out? But before Coburg we must and will see each other. We'll make great plans.*

When Kaufmann is thinking of kisses and embraces, and how he scratched Inge's face with his stubble in Italy, he calls himself her *wild man* or her *black man*. It sounds like an affectionate threat, as if he were reminding them both of endearments that she herself whispered to him as they kissed and embraced. *I hope I won't forget my shaving kit for Stockholm*, he writes shortly before leaving. More difficulties do come up at the last moment. The steamer he was going to take to Gotland has suffered storm damage and has no room for a passenger. But thanks to a lucky coincidence there's a substitute in view. The very next day a ship is to leave Gdingen not for Gotland but, much better, for Stockholm itself. They can spend more days together in Stockholm than on Gotland. Writing hastily in pencil during the journey, he sends her a message from Marienburg station on the border between East Prussia and Danzig, telling her when he will arrive and saying that he will phone as soon as he does. He adds: *I have my shaving kit with me!!!*

Rudolf Kaufmann spends five days with Ingeborg Magnusson in Stockholm. He arrives on a Wednesday and leaves on the following Monday. He writes no letters to her during this time. He starts writing again only when he is in Coburg.

Ingeborg Magnusson (right) with her sister Greta

A week ago today we were going out to Drottningholm on that lovely Sunday in fall, just the two of us. It was so beautiful. And that afternoon and evening we were entirely together that one last time, we forgot everything that parted us and now parts us again. I feel as if a whole month had passed since I held my Inge in my arms, scratching her mouth and her whole face with my stubble. I've seen and heard and come to know so much that's new since then. Yet I'm still re-living those wonderful days in Stockholm, when we were one in body and soul, really man and wife, moglie e marito, man och fru.*
It's a bond that will enclose us entirely and never let us go again.

Kaufmann does not return to Königsberg from Stockholm, but goes straight to Coburg. He feels uneasy when the train stops in his old university town of Greifswald, and he doesn't get out to go and visit teachers, former fellow students, colleagues of the old days. But there's an old friend waiting for him on the platform in Berlin, another unemployed scientist, for whom science is now *only poetry*. Over knuckle of pork and sauerkraut, and then as they drink red country wine in the Ristorante Italiano, Jim tells Rudolf his plans. He's going to open a graphology salon, and hopes to earn plenty of money that way.

The rest of the journey is long and tedious. Kaufmann is tired when he arrives in Coburg. Once again, there's more between him and her now than deep water—there's the land mass itself, and even more trouble than before. Kaufmann is moving to the middle of the German Reich, to Coburg, close to the border of Bavaria and Thuringia. To Coburg, of all places, the first German city whose citizens elected a Nazi as their mayor. And did it as early as 1929.

---

* "Man and wife" in Italian and Swedish, respectively.

The house stands in a very, very beautiful large park. The headmaster is really nice. Besides gymnastics I'll be teaching geography, biology, physics, and art. There are 2 more teachers, and a total of 43 pupils, all of them nice, bright boys and girls. Besides getting free board and lodging, and my laundry done for me, I'll be earning 65 Reichsmarks a month. Which is better than nothing. The pupils have all taken to me. Even though I'm such a wild, brutal man!!!!

The pupils of the Preacher Hirsch Boarding School.
In the last row, on the left, Hermann Hirsch;
on the right, looking at the ground, Rudolf Kaufmann.

Well, I've already settled in here in Coburg. I'm popular with the pupils, indispensable to the headmaster. I think that when it comes to the contract I'll ask for a little more, perhaps a salary of 100 instead of 65 Reichsmarks as well as the free board and lodging. But all this must be very diplomatically handled.

It's a shame you can't see and meet all my little friends here, "Tobacco," "Cuddly," "Clumsy," "Fatty," "Hippo," "Schlomo," and the rest, with their various names and nicknames.

There'll be great excitement this afternoon, because a movie is going to be screened here, The Eleven Devils, a football film with Gustav Fröhlich—some say I look like him—and blonde Evelin Holt, real name Edith Sklarz, who was actually at this boarding school years ago. They've garlanded a picture of her when she was a little schoolgirl and hung it up. Since the film is a silent movie, our school musicians will provide the accompaniment. Coburg has its own excitement today, because "the Führer" is here to dedicate a memorial.

Coburg celebrates under swastika banners waving in the breeze, while the pupils and teachers of the Preacher Hirsch Boarding School keep to themselves. Apartheid functions on the large scale and the small scale alike. The appointment of Rudolf Kaufmann to his post as a sports teacher seems to be all part of it. The Nazis are not yet seriously contemplating the physical extermination of Jews. The methods they use against them are expulsion, boycott, financial ruin, the mobilization of envy and malice, wagging tongues, greed, public humiliation, official harassment, intimidation, banning them from certain professions, threats, exclusion, the expulsion of "Jewish" children from "German" schools. At this time Jewish schools can expect a certain amount of goodwill from the authorities. When Hermann Hirsch, preacher to the Jewish community in Coburg, wants to turn his boarding school (which is well known even outside the city itself) into a private school, permission is not refused, and during the year 1935 the number of pupils rises from twenty-eight to forty-three.

That is why Rudolf Kaufmann received such a prompt answer to his advertisement.

I'm on the go from morning to night. But I enjoy the work. You can do so much good to the little creatures. They have a real home here. They're tremendously respectful to me. Every evening at bedtime I have to check (1) whether their clothes are tidily put away, (2) whether their fingernails are clean, (3) whether they've washed their feet, and (4) whether they've washed their ears. It's an idea I introduced myself. I'm regarded as a perfect example of discipline and order—I, of all people, who was considered a perfect example of disorder at home. . . .

Today was such a lovely sunny day that we had lunch out of doors. It tasted wonderful. Exercising does me so much good. I'm growing, blossoming, flourishing. I still haven't developed the Skansen photos. I'll do it now. I hope they've turned out all right. On Sunday I'm taking the football team to Nuremberg. We're going to play a big match there. Everyone's very excited.

In early November it's as if summer were coming back to Franconia again. One Sunday, Kaufmann goes to the nearby valley of the river Main. He takes a long walk, starting at Stauffenstein, and Inge—so he writes next day, and she can read his letter two days later in Stockholm—is with him.

. . . and then we went uphill to the Fourteen Saints pilgrimage church. It was rather like S. Luca. So were the plain and the mountain slope. Then we went on through the woods, and I had to kiss you behind every tree.

There's no one else on the outing with them apart from Viktor von Scheffel,* whose song, says Kaufmann, *we sing so much in Germany.* "The sky is pure that meets our gaze, we'll rust if we sit long. The brightest of fine, sunlit days let's greet with merry song. A wandering scholar I will be, with pilgrim's staff in hand, and in the summer I will see our dear Franconian land. . . . I climb St. Veit of Staffelstein, and down below me lies the country round the river Main, spread out before my eyes. From Grabfeldgau to Bamberg fair, with meadows, rivers, springs— mountains and hills rise in the air, ah, would that I had wings!" Kaufmann wishes he could grow wings too, but the wish remains only a wish. His thoughts and his letters alone grow wings in this story. That evening Kaufmann is back with his pupils.

I have to play "Ghosts" with them every evening. It means scuffling with them in the dark, always against five or six at once. I really have to defend myself if I'm to win. Then I tickle some of them until they're all laughing so much that they give in. I sometimes lose against the larger boys—a number of them are heavier than me. I'm so glad that I have work now, and I can forget any stupid thoughts. For everything is so bleak these days. Almost all the pupils' parents have had to sell their businesses at knockdown prices. And so it goes on. But I don't want to write about all this. If only I could earn enough to keep us both—two young people who long for each other so much. If you had a job here yourself we could manage that very soon. I keep thinking it over this way and that.

It is possible that the idea of moving to Germany, where he suddenly has prospects again, doesn't even strike her as rash or outlandish. Most people in Sweden still admire the neighbor-

*Viktor von Scheffel, 1826–1886, wrote this patriotic song about Franconia in 1859. It has nine verses in all.

ing country of Germany on the other side of the Baltic for its achievements and its culture. To Swedish ears, much of what is now being said and written about conditions in the German Reich, particularly what emigrants say in explanation of their arrival in the north, sounds very much like pessimistic exaggeration. Kaufmann never exaggerates in his letters. Nor is he pessimistic. He prefers to leave things out, he plays with ideas, sees opportunities even where none exist. But the idea that Inge might visit him in Coburg over Christmas doesn't have to remain a dream. That can be arranged.

If you could bring some butter and cake from Sweden that would be wonderful. There's very little butter here, because Germany has to buy metal ore instead, which is quite right, and not a single German will complain. We can get hold of snowshoes somewhere. You'll probably arrive at a quarter to seven on Sunday evening. I'll be there to meet you, of course, beaming with joy. I don't yet know just where you'll be staying overnight, but we'll go on again on Monday morning, because Coburg is a small town grown too large, and there are reasons why I don't want people talking about me too much. I do hope the headmaster will be kind enough to let us spend the New Year together. But we'll be glad of every hour we can be with each other. School finishes on Thursday evening. There's going to be a gymnastics display and a theatrical performance for the end of term. We're rehearsing hard.

So after their two days in Bologna and their five days in Stockholm together, Rudolf Kaufmann and Ingeborg Magnusson have another six days at Christmas, spent at Neuhaus in the Thuringian Forest, staying in a private furnished room with the use of a kitchen. It is an isolated place, just what they want.

On New Year's Eve, Ingeborg is back in Stockholm, and Kaufmann is alone again. In the first week of January 1936 he says goodbye to his sister Liese, who is leaving Germany with her husband.

I'm going to Erfurt this afternoon to see them one last time before they leave for Palestine. I have a vague feeling that my own path may lead me there some time. It's really funny. Once I'd simply have laughed at the idea, but now I see it quite differently. Anti-Semitism is a fact, and it travels the world along with the emigrants. Sooner or later it turns up everywhere. The only place where we're regarded as belonging is Palestine. And yet I felt German, and it's difficult for me to adjust my ideas. I'll be interested to hear how my sister settles in there. I hope all the plans she and her husband are making will work out. They're both gardeners.

Last summer in Georgenswalde, soon after his return from Italy, Kaufmann was still writing about "*our* coast" and "*our* beautiful Baltic Sea" in his letters. Now, it seems, his sense of being German belongs to the past, and he speaks of it in the past imperfect tense. But as the son of an Evangelical professor of physics, and baptized in the Evangelical faith himself, he does not feel that Jewish identity is a foundation that he can build on; it seems almost hopelessly strange, an imposition. When he first tells Inge that he is going to study the language he might find useful for a future in Palestine, he makes a spelling mistake, writing not *Hebräisch*, the German form of the word, but *Hebreisch*, more like the English spelling.

I'm starting to learn Hebrew now. I may need it some day. No one knows that. However, it's a difficult language. I'd never have thought of learning something like that before.

There is a note of depression in the letters that Rudolf Kaufmann sends to Stockholm early in 1936. The photographic enlarger that he is constructing in his spare time, so that he can reproduce the pictures of his days with Inge in the Thuringian Forest in the format they deserve, is making progress. But what he calls "stupid ideas" come thick and fast now, and often get the upper hand.

Away from the world here, there's so much time to think and to brood on fate. It's so different from when I was in the hustle and bustle of life. I think we poor creatures have a lot to endure yet. Don't be cross or even sad when I write like this. I often feel as if my path and that of many others must lead us back to Judaism, whether that's what we want or not. I think a great deal about this. Because the only openings in life that I see for myself are in a Jewish life. It's an ancient fate, we're predestined to it, and this isn't the first time it's happened. What did I ever guess of all this in the old days? I was just a man like anyone else, I felt as German as my comrades. At heart, I didn't feel it was anything to do with me. My problems were to do with rocks, nature, sport, art, sometimes women, but never the fate of a great many people. My own fate was something I couldn't yet foresee, and as it slowly unfurled everything about it fascinated me. I've always studied myself like a natural scientist, I've been my own psychologist. But now I feel as if my life and my fate tie me to a group that I've always belonged to because of my blood without really knowing it. It's no good struggling against that fate. It all seems to be preordained by providence. Oh, Inge, why does a human being have to be pigeonholed at the moment of birth? And there's the question of race and all the stuff I used to laugh at so much. But it's serious, because fate has made it serious. What will our future be like? I don't see any opportunities for myself outside Judaism. And that would make it impossible for the two of us ever to be together. There'll be the same ideas about race there as everywhere else. I used to think so little about such things, and recently they've been on my mind so much. Inge, I can see your tears coming when you read all this. I feel the same. Yet we can't close our eyes to it. Life is so hard. It's only when good fortune brings us together for a while that we can briefly forget everything else, just be two human beings, that's all. Inge, forgive me for writing all this. You understand everything about me. I can see the years passing with no hope of a home where we can live together as a couple, where our children can play with friends. In times like these our love alone won't see us through. And yet, Ingelein, perhaps we're fortunate creatures after all. Perhaps those few moments together outweigh all the lonely hours in life. Think how much love and happiness we've known because we met. Life usually goes on so monotonously, with so little love in it—so how happy it makes us to have had those few short hours together. Ours was a fairy-tale happiness in the snow. Unforgettable hours. I hope, oh, I do hope we can have more such hours this summer. How? I don't know yet. But it must be possible. The strength of that "must" hasn't left us yet.

Life is busy in the boarding school. Reports on the pupils have to be typed out and sent to their parents every month. The Jewish holiday of Purim at the beginning of March is celebrated with a theatrical show. Inge in Stockholm knows nothing about Purim, and the way Kaufmann explains it to her suggests that he himself has acquired his knowledge of the subject only recently:

It's been celebrated since the time of the captivity in Persia and Babylon. The young King Ahasuerus of Persia chose the most beautiful woman he could find to be queen of his harem, and her name was Esther (she was Jewish). It all sounds like a fairy tale from the Thousand and One Nights. But Haman, the young Persian minister, told the king: "There is a people that ignores your gods and your laws. You must destroy them!" So Haman sent messengers to the satraps in every country, telling them that all the Jews were to be killed on a certain day. The king didn't know about Esther's origins, but she revealed them to him, and reminded him of the good things that representatives of her people had done for him. So the Jews were saved, and the villains were hanged on the gallows.

Kaufmann would like to go to Stockholm at Easter, but his money won't stretch that far. However, he intends to go to Sweden in the summer and stay as long as possible, perhaps do a little geological research, manufacture work for himself *trilobitizing*, and Inge could give him a hand. Just possibly Professor Stensiö might sponsor his research. It's worth asking again. He also writes to Sven Hedin once more, having seen him from a distance at a lecture in Coburg. When Kaufmann thinks of geology, his independent research, work in the field, it occurs to him that he doesn't want to be a teacher permanently, that he's living a kind of monastic life in the boarding school these days, hardly mingling with the world at all. So he is not tempted by the offer of a teaching job at a boarding school in Florence. One reason is that the salary is only 150 lire, but the main one is that Florence is the wrong way for him to go. After all, there's a similar school in Skåne. He will write to *that* school, and Inge must cross her fingers for him.

At the end of March, Kaufmann has an unexpected visit from his eldest brother. The two haven't seen each other for four years. Albert is an engineer and lives in Cologne with his wife Helene. He too has had a hard time. He too has found new prospects opening up recently. He has *"invented a dust-shield, and is on the way to success."*

At the beginning of April, the school year ends with the usual flurry of activity: there are marks to be awarded, meetings to be held, reports to be written. Sven Hedin sends a friendly answer to Kaufmann's letter. He can't find him work, he often receives similar applications, and is very sorry that he can't help all these people. Kaufmann is twenty-seven on 3 April. Two days before, he realizes that he doesn't know when Inge's birthday is. He has forgotten the exact date of their meeting in Italy, too. *Help me!* he writes, meaning that he wants her to jog his memory. It is spring in Franconia. Kaufmann is exercising to keep fit again, and is proud of achieving 1.45 to 1.50 meters in the high jump in the new pit in the grounds of the boarding school, as well as doing 5.85 meters in the long jump, and to the delight of his pupils he does that daredevil leap, a free *salto mortale*, in his "old age"—for he has the beginnings of a little bald patch already.

In the Easter vacation he visits his father in Freiburg, goes for long walks in the Black Forest (in his mind, with Inge to keep him company), explores his father's library, and reads treatises on the theory of relativity and on quantum physics. He helps in the house, cooking and washing up, and often plays with his two-year-old half brother.

I have such fun with my little brother. He's a dear little fellow. He's 2 years old and still sees the world as very new and overwhelming. I often play with him, and then he laughs and says, "Rudolf." He's a good gymnast already and we do exercises together. Of course he's an infant prodigy. That's only to be expected of a Kaufmann.

Rudolf Kaufmann's father married again after his first wife's death in 1928. According to the present law and the language used by the Nazis, Else is Aryan, but her marriage to Walter Kaufmann took place in 1932, so it is not a criminal offence under the new law of 1935. However, Walter's anxiety and shortness of temper have become more marked over the years. He takes less and less notice of his grown-up children. It is as if he wanted to protect his new family from the old one.

The new school year begins in early May, in wonderful spring weather. Kaufmann teaches out of doors most of the time: athletics, art, natural history. In the evenings he and his colleague Edel go cross-country running in the woods and hills around Coburg. He has a new javelin. He trains hard with it on the grounds of the boarding school, and soon he can throw a full 45 meters, as he could in the past.

It's nice for the boys here too in this huge park. We go cycling on the sports ground in the evenings, with me in charge, weaving along in lines that keep scattering. We all enjoy it. At the same time, of course, they study hard. It really isn't easy to keep control over so many Jewish boys. They're very temperamental and self-willed. You have to be energetic, stern and patient with them. In return, they understand lessons quickly and are really interested. They bring me everything they can find: beetles, butterflies, lizards, frogs, mice, salamanders, etc. I like teaching natural history best of all, because the grounds contain everything the children need to observe.

But some of the opportunities offered on the grounds are there only of necessity. The new sandpit for high-jumping and long-jumping, for instance, was put in because Jewish children and their teachers are no longer allowed to use public sports fields in Coburg, and at a large athletics meeting in mid-June they compete only among themselves.

On Sunday your little husband went to the athletics meeting in Nuremberg with six of the boys. You can be very proud of me. I shared most of the prizes with a probable competitor in the Olympics (a probable German competitor, even though he's Jewish). I came second in the javelin, discus, rock tossing, third in the 800 meters and third in the six-sports event (110 m, 800 m, high jump, long jump, shot-putting, the discus). And ten minutes after the 800 m, in which the Olympic contender collapsed, I ran the 5000 m cool as you please, coming in sixth, not at all strained. There was a lot of applause for me. I threw the discus 29 m, and the rock (weighing 16.5. kg) 7.18 m. Our boys did very well too. Summer has come at last. I saw glowworms again this evening! Oh, I thought of S. Luca so much. We go around in the sun from 2 to 4 and splash about in the fountain. Unfortunately the boys can't use the public swimming pool. I'm really brown already.

Inge has told him the missing dates of the calendar of their "marriage" to each other, so he can underline the number 5 in his letter of 5 June 1936 twice.

So much has happened since this time last year—the day that turned my life in a new direction, back to the north! Back to the countries where, inside me, I really belong, back to the people I understand and who understand me. I found my happiness then, and it was you.

Since then they have spent thirteen days together, two in Bologna and Venice, five in Stockholm, six in Coburg. Now they want to meet again in the summer, whether or not Professor Stensiö is willing to contribute research funds. They are still not sure when Inge can take her vacation. But as Kaufmann's school vacation lasts from mid-July until early September, he can adjust to her arrangements. They are not sure, either, how he can pay for his visit to Sweden. It is not that he is short of money, but money can still be taken outside the Reich only in amounts of ten marks a month, not enough for him to travel abroad.

So there is a good deal in Kaufmann's letters about the tiresome *denaro*. The Italian that he has so far used to express tender emotions, and initially also to add last-minute comments on the envelope, now serves mainly to disguise his comments on the currency restrictions, a code for whole passages of information about problems with passports and cash. They must all be solved so that he can go to see her. His sister Trude in Copenhagen has given him a tip: anyone traveling to Denmark can put in an application to take 140 Reichsmarks. So Kaufmann tries to get a letter of credit for Denmark. However, there is a snag. His passport still gives Bologna as his permanent place of residence—so he is regarded as a German living abroad, and as such he can't get a letter of credit. It would be possible to change his passport and have Coburg entered as his new place of residence. But as all the Jews in Coburg have had their passports confiscated, he is afraid that then he will lose his too, and with it any prospect of a summer in Sweden. Inge will be able to advance him some money, and he will return it on her next visit to Coburg. His sister Trude in Copenhagen can lend him something too. And he may be able to buy train tickets here in Germany for both of them, for the whole of the planned round trip. It will all work out somehow. His confidence, the sense of that imperative *must*, does not desert him even in early July when, three weeks before he plans to travel, he has an accident.

Would you believe it, I stupidly fell doing the high jump and twisted my body the opposite way from my left foot. So I suffered the well-known typical skier's injury. It hurt, of course. Luckily the doctor pushed at my leg—like a butcher—until the bones were straight again, so now, two days later, I'm quite myself again, and I'm already limping around on my bandaged foot. It doesn't hurt anymore either. I'm glad about that, and I keep cheerful, because I know that by the time of our vacation, when we'll see each other, I'll be quite all right again. I'm already with you in my mind, and everything would be fine if it wasn't for that stupid denaro. Today I finally had a negative decision from Stensiö: "Very sorry to have to say that in the present state of the economy . . . but next year . . . "

His foot takes longer than expected to heal. Limping as he is, he can't even go into the center of Coburg to buy himself a better pen. Inge will have to puzzle out his illegible handwriting. His plan is to set off from Coburg around 1 August, going first to Berlin. He wants to visit his friend Jim there, and consult a good doctor about his leg, and if he can still get a ticket maybe he will see something of the Olympic Games, which begin on 2 August, a Sunday. A few days later he will go on to join her. He is eager to start the journey, he writes.

Luckily it's only a few days now until I leave. I can hardly wait! I'm glad to say that my knee is doing very well again. I can already walk long distances without getting tired, and without anything showing. But it will probably be a little while yet before I'm fully mobile. Credo di non avere più bisogno del D. Perquè avro centocinquanta. Nel caso di dovere avere più posso mandare dopo colla mia sorella e pretare un poco da te.[*] *I'm delighted to hear that you have found me a good, cheap place to stay in Stockholm. Thank you with all my heart. You're a real magician, finding that! We'll have such a wonderful few days together that we'll never want to part again. Yes, I'm really looking forward to seeing the Skagerak coast at Göteborg. I've read so much about it. Walking among those lonely, rounded rocks, worn smooth by the sea, will be just what the two of us enjoy. In my next letter I'll tell you my exact time of arrival. I think it will be on or around 5.8. Then we can be together in the evenings on your last few days at work.*

Rudolf Kaufmann writes this letter on 29 July 1936, and by the time Ingeborg receives it that final week of waiting is half over. Another letter is to come, telling her his precise time of arrival—and then he'll be there himself. But the promised letter never arrives, and nor does he, not on 5 August or on any of the days that follow. Ingeborg waits in vain. It is a bad week for her. On 10 August she writes a letter to Denmark, to Kaufmann's sister Trude and her husband, the geologist Curt Teichert.

---

[*] "I think I shall not need any more denaro now. I shall have a hundred and fifty. If I do need more I can send to my sister later and borrow a little from you."

Dear Frau and Herr Teichert,

Rudolf has not arrived, and I think some accident must have happened to him. He wrote on 29 July from Coburg to say he would be in Sthlm on 5 August (or around then). He was going to let me know exactly what day and time he would arrive. I have not heard anything. I would be very grateful if you could write by return of post and tell me if you know where Rudolf is, and if he is all right. I am very anxious.

With best wishes . . .

Charlottenlund, 11.8.36

Dear Fräulein Magnusson,

We received your express letter this morning on our return home from several weeks staying on Bornholm. I immediately telegraphed the Hirsch School in Coburg and asked for information on Rudolf's whereabouts. But at the moment there seems to be no one there to answer a telegram. We heard this afternoon that the telegram has been sent on to Herr Hirsch in Montreux, where it seems he is spending his vacation. So at the moment we don't know what else we can do, and of course we ourselves are very anxious. Please write and let us know at once if Rudolf has arrived in Stockholm after all. Meanwhile, I hope to hear from Herr Hirsch too, and then we can think what else to do. In my own turn, I will let you know. Rudolf is sometimes rather thoughtless. So we may hope that if he hasn't told you about some reason for postponing his visit, then he's just idling around somewhere.

My wife joins me in sending best wishes ...

Stockholm 12.8.36

Dear Frau and Herr Teichert,

Rudolf still hasn't arrived. He would certainly have let me know if he hadn't been able to come at the time we agreed. He was going to trav-el to Berlin on 1 August and see a doctor there for his injured leg. I am on vacation now, and if you have no objection I will travel to Copenhagen tomorrow evening, arriving at 22.35. I can't rest here. I think Rudolf must have had some kind of accident. I hope, I do hope everything will turn out all right.

With best wishes . . .

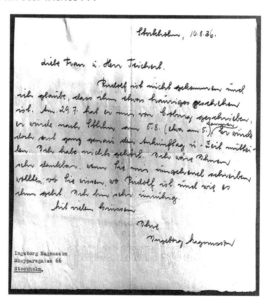

Newspaper readers in Coburg know by now what kind of acci-dent Rudolf Kaufmann has had. On 1 August, a day before the beginning of the summer Olympic Games, the local newspaper, the *Bayerische Ostmark – Coburger Nationalzeitung*, published the following report:

"ARRESTED FOR OFFENSES AGAINST THE RACE LAWS. TYPI-CAL CASE OF JEWISH EFFRONTERY IN COBURG. 27-year-old

Jewish athletics teacher Rudolf Kaufmann, of Coburg, has been arrested for contravention of Paragraphs 2 and 5 of the Law for the Protection of German Blood and German Honor.

Kaufmann met a young widow, a resident of Neuses, at a local dance hall in May, and became friendly with her. Their acquaintanceship led to sexual intercourse, with serious consequences for Kaufmann, who realized after a while that he had symptoms of venereal disease. Kaufmann went for treatment to a local doctor who specializes in such diseases . . . The illegal relations between the Jew Kaufmann and the young Aryan woman came to light when Kaufmann told the doctor who had presumably infected him. Thereupon both parties were taken into police custody.

The chief blame in this case undoubtedly lies with the man. In order to achieve his ends, the Jew Kaufmann *deliberately* concealed his racial origins from the woman. It is clear that he intended to make her his victim from the fact that he identified himself to his acquaintance (only after some time) as 'Rudolf Kaufmann, a geologist at present visiting Coburg.' Since Kaufmann is not strikingly Jewish in appearance, the widow never suspected his race. She has been released from custody, while Kaufmann is being held until his trial for contravention of the race laws. Since he has close connections with Sweden, it was feared that he might try to escape.

This incident shows yet again the effrontery with which the Jew seeks out his victim, even today when the National Socialist state has passed strict laws to protect the Aryan race, and our German National Comrades are sufficiently well informed."

Reinhard Kaiser

Coburg, 13.8.1936

Dear Ingelein,

I have to write you a letter which will cause you terrible grief; I can never make up for it. I did write ten days ago, but now I've had to rewrite the letter because I wanted to confess everything but I couldn't, I'd gone into far too much detail. I can picture your dreadful anxiety and the distress you must have suffered these last two weeks, getting no news when you were expecting me to arrive in St. as your guest. I was unfaithful to you just once, in a rash moment, two and a half months ago; it made me unwell for a while then, but that's how I came to be arrested two weeks ago and am now in custody on remand. I daren't ask you to forgive me. I was going to confess it all to you in Sweden. But now it's too late. I'm not worthy of you anymore and I beg you to try to forget me. Thank you for the true, pure love you gave me. You were so good to me, and I proved weak, and now I must pay for it. I had been feeling so lonely here, without any friends of my own age, and so I was weak back in May. I am so sad for you, because you have been so badly deceived in me. And you too were looking forward to our vacation together, which can never come to anything now. Don't grieve too much, I will bear my fate with composure, whatever it may be. So much has been taken from me during my life, my mother, my chosen profession, and much else that I loved. But this time I failed out of thoughtlessness, and must endure whatever happens to me. And I can do nothing, nothing for you, only think of you and be grateful for everything. Forget me, because I have brought shame on you and everyone.

Your Rudolf.

Coburg District Court, remand prisoner R.K.

This letter is in an unusually small envelope lined with thin, multicolored tissue paper, and unlike all the others it is written not on plain white paper but on a sheet of salmon-pink deckle-edged notepaper with a watermark, a pattern of irregular rhombus shapes across the whole sheet, looking as if they were sketched there loosely with a brush. It is possible that a cell-mate gave Kaufmann this elegant notepaper and envelope. They seem strangely out of place. Of all the letters that Rudolf Kaufmann wrote Ingeborg Magnusson, this most resembles the usual idea of a love letter in its outward appearance.

Inge Magnusson does not forget the man she met over a year ago in Italy, and with whom she has spent no more than thirteen days since. She forgives him for his infidelity, if "infidelity" and "forgive" are the right words in the circumstances. She stands by him. She goes on writing to him. Kaufmann's "close connections with Sweden" are maintained. By now even the Coburg press knows about those connections. It may be that at the time of Kaufmann's arrest the police came upon Inge's letters, and perhaps the travel brochures she had sent him in May. She had underlined some of the particularly tempting offers in them in red.

In the time after Kaufmann's arrest, Inge Magnusson gets to know his family better, exchanging a number of letters with his brother Hans and Hans's wife Vera, who emigrate to England that fall. She also visits Kaufmann's sister Trude and her husband in Copenhagen. Perhaps she already guesses that she will soon have to rely on Rudolf Kaufmann's immediate family members if her contact with him is not to be broken. At first, however, letters still travel unhindered between Stockholm and Coburg, although under the eye of the prison censor.

Thank you with all my heart for your dear letter. And I was so glad to hear that you have been to see Curt and Trude, and have met them both in Copenhagen. So you have not been as lonely as I feared. I can well imagine the impression that the beautiful beech woods of Denmark made on you. There are few things as lovely as a beech wood when the sun shines down on it and the ground is all dappled light and shade. But just now I'm imagining how lovely it must be at present in Stockholm too, in Drottningholm and Skansen. They're all like little bits of paradise, especially on clear fall days. After the case comes to court I expect I'll only be able to write to Father and my brothers and sisters, but there's some time to go yet. And then I'll ask Trude to send my letters on to you. I'm all right here. I like sawing wood best. And I'm studying in my old textbooks, and I mean to practise shorthand. . . . The people at the boarding school are so concerned about me that I feel quite ashamed. Inge, I'm happy and grateful that in spite of everything you don't despise me. I hope I can thank you and make it up to you some day.

On 10 December 1936, the criminal chamber of the Coburg courts finds Rudolf Kaufmann guilty of offenses against the racial laws, and condemns him to three years in prison minus the four months already spent on remand, with five years' revocation of his civil rights. During the trial the public prosecutor points out that if the legislation of the German nation doesn't suit the defendant, he ought either to have stayed abroad, where he had spent some time, or have gone back there. Kaufmann is defended by an attorney from Bamberg, Thomas Dehler, who after the war was the Federal Republic's Minister of Justice from 1953 to 1956, and later was leader of the Free Democratic Party, as well as acting as its parliamentary party chairman in the Bundestag. Dehler has hated the Nazis for a long time. He has several times represented Jews in civil cases, and his defense of Rudolf Kaufmann earns him a report in early 1937 in the notorious *Der Stürmer*, edited by Julius Streicher, "The German Weekly Journal in the Struggle for the Truth."

Letter from Thomas Dehler to Curt Teichert, dated 10 December 1936, apparently written immediately after the end of Rudolf Kaufmann's trial:
"Dear Dr Teichert: It has been a wearing trial, with a terrible result: three years in prison (less four months' remand custody), five years' loss of civil rights. I will try appealing. R.K. bears it bravely and sends his good wishes. Most sincerely, Dehler."

OFFENSE AGAINST THE RACE LAWS IN COBURG. THE JEW KAUFMANN CONDEMNED TO 3 YEARS IN PRISON / DR DEHLER FROM BAMBERG A COMRADE OF THE JEWS.

"... The defense of the Jew who offended against the race laws was in the hands of the *non-Jewish* attorney Dr. Dehler of Bamberg. He is married to the Jewess Frank from Bad Kissingen. He was trained in Bamberg, in the chambers of the

Jewish attorney Werner, who has emigrated. Between them, his wife and his 'teacher' helped to make the German attorney Dehler a true comrade of the Jews. No Jew could have acted in more Jewish a manner than Dehler did in court. Citing a whole collection of evidence, he sought to show that the defendant was 'a highly intelligent and educated man of the finest character.' His action, said Dehler, could be ascribed only to a 'moment of weakness.' Furthermore, Dr. Dehler said something about the defendant's 'genuine remorse,' and asked for a lenient sentence. The court was not impressed by the idle talk of Dehler, that comrade of the Jews.... Attorneys like Dehler, who for the sake of money can bring themselves to defend what the state has declared to be a crime, are men of low character and deserve to be struck off the list."

Der Stürmer, *No. 4, 1937*

The single surviving fragment of all the letters from Ingeborg Magnusson to Rudolf Kaufmann was probably also written some time just after sentence was passed. It is a sheet of squared paper, undated, found among his correspondence with her, and is clearly a draft for a Christmas letter.

Dearest R.,

I have heard all about it from Trude. We have a hard time ahead of us, but I promise you to be brave, just as you are being brave. Knowing that will help us both. It will be a long time before we can see each other again, but if we can't write to each other meanwhile that won't change anything. It will all stay the way it always has been. You'll hear news of me from Trude. Now, you must be pleased: on the first day of Christmas I'm going to stay with Trude and Curt. I am so glad and happy, because I feel that Trude likes me. She writes that "she would really love to have me with them." Aren't you pleased about that? I'm going to stay with them for over a week. I have had a sweet Christmas letter from Hans and Vera. They are well and thinking of you a lot.

It's a year ago tomorrow that I went to see my good friends in northern Sweden. That was my best Christmas ever. We went through the white woods on snowshoes every day, and up to the mountains. It was a dream of snow and sunlight. I've probably told you about it before, but you know how it is, if you've had a lovely experience you want to keep on talking and thinking about it. I'll never forget those days.

At the moment it's not very Christmassy here in Sthlm. It's raining, and the temperature is +8° in the shade. We always usually get a little snow on Christmas Eve, so we hope it will be the same this year. The climate here is starting to get unbearable. The good Marchese has gone back to his own country to get new forces. My family are well and send you heartfelt Christmas greetings. All of us who love you will be with you in our minds at Christmas, as usual. Dear Rudolf, there's so much that I wanted to say to you. But you understand me even without words. You mustn't grieve on my behalf, I'll always stay the same and be brave, as I have promised. You must

promise me the same. Goodbye, lilleman*, and heartfelt greetings
from your Ingeb.

Relying on the secret understanding between them, Inge
Magnusson "moves" Thuringia to the Arctic Circle. It is possible that her letter crossed with Kaufmann's of 21 December
1936, in which he assumes the same understanding and
reminds her of last year's snow.

Dear Ingelein,
    I was very, very glad to get your last letter. You'll have heard
about my situation by now. Don't be too sad, Ingelein. I'm all right
otherwise, and I have great hopes of the appeal. But one must bear
one's fate patiently, whatever happens. Yes, you're quite right to say
that some good can be found in everything if one is "romantic" and
optimistic at heart. If I do have to stay here several years I hope I can
learn a good trade, for instance as a project manager in the construc-
tion trade, a joiner, or something else. I know many people who have
been looking for a chance to learn a trade for a long time, wanting to
change careers, but they couldn't find a master craftsman to take
them on. However, there won't be any such problems for me. You see
how there's always a silver lining. . . . The winter hasn't started here
yet. Anyone wanting to ski in the Thuringian Forest this Christmas
wouldn't get his money's worth. I'd so much have liked to make you
something nice as a present, like last year. Unfortunately I didn't
have time. While the appeal is still pending, and there could be a
wait of over three months, you can write to me as often as you like.

The book about South America in the Christmas parcel sent

---

* Swedish, "little husband."

from Copenhagen by Curt and Trude offers views of a free and distant world of questionable charm. Kaufmann's two cellmates are particularly amazed by the natural yellow of the Danish cake and butter that emerge from the rustling wrapping paper. Hans and Vera send Christmas greetings from London too. Now that they are struggling with the English language, they are really impressed by the perfect German in which Inge corresponds with them. Kaufmann enters the New Year of 1937 as if "dormant." That, he writes, is the best way to start it and get through it. But he also knows how to make use of his time in prison, and is returning to the subject for which he had no leisure while he was a teacher: geology. He begins a new essay on his beloved trilobites while he is in remand custody in Coburg.

Yes, it's really true, I'm immersed in trilobites again, and am fascinated by them. I am writing a new essay in which I put my statistical findings about the trilobites to theoretical use. It's primarily in answer to the work of a German geologist in Berlin, confirming it. He has brought out a new book and often cites my work, acknowledging its value. I have been writing full speed ahead for a week now, and time is suddenly going really fast. I've scarcely finished a drawing or a chapter before the day is over, and I feel sorry that it's dark already. It used to be quite different. I realize now that my work is gradually getting better known, and I am very proud of that. . . . You see I have plenty to do now, and for weeks ahead. So I'm glad that I have nothing to distract me. I don't need to worry about how to keep myself at the moment, and get everything I need. . . . We often play a board game here; it's fun. It's called "Mensch ärgere dich nicht!"* That really suits us. It helps to pass the time very quickly.

---

* A traditional German board game a little like ludo, but the title means, "Don't get annoyed!"

On 12 February 1937 Kaufmann's appeal is rejected by the Reich Appeals court in Leipzig. A few days later he is allowed to write Inge one more letter—the last for a long time.

My appeal has been thrown out in Leipzig, so I expect I'll soon be moved to a regular prison, probably in Amberg. Don't be too sad, Ingelein. I may have part of my sentence remitted for good conduct. You don't need to worry about me. You know me too well for that. I've already suffered so many blows of fate, and I haven't been crushed. Far from it. I can still take things equally, and I have my sense of humour. And I know you're like me in that. Of course being parted from each other seems terribly hard. But you said yourself that there's something good and enjoyable to be found in the smallest little everyday events. And that's the way we two are. Life in the regular prison will be much more pleasant than the time I spent on remand. Even the food is quite different. But first and foremost there's regular work, and that's the main thing. Because that way time passes in a flash, you hardly know how. I'm going to sign up to the building trade there. And there'll be intellectual stimulation, good books, language teaching, gymnastics, and all sorts of other things. I'm just so sorry for you, my piccola moglie.* Because you'll have to wait so long. . . . I'm glad I've been able to start on my scientific work again. I hope I can finish the essay while I'm still here. Or perhaps I can finish it later. If you want to hear news of me, then ask Dr Dehler, the attorney, No. 4 Sophienstrasse, Bamberg. I will think of you and love you all the time. That will be a comfort to you too. Ingelein, write here just once more, and then go on writing to the other prison. As far as I know letters from outside can come in. And even if I can't reply myself, you'll know without words what I want

---

* Italian, "little wife."

to say to you and how much I want to thank you. We shall be entirely together in our thoughts. Be my brave lille fru.* And I will be brave too. And one day we'll be together again and no one will come between us. Goodbye, Ingelein, I know you will keep me in your heart and I'll keep you in mine.

Love and kisses with all my heart.

Your piccolo marito,† Rudolf

P.S. The day of my release is 12 October 1939.

At first Rudolf Kaufmann can write letters from Amberg prison only to members of his family: he corresponds with his father in Freiburg, who sends copies of his letters on to his brother and sister, Hans in London and Trude in Copenhagen, and they in turn send them on to Ingeborg Magnusson.

Dear Father,

    . . . I have been given permission to learn English. Unfortunately, I didn't get permission to write treatises and so on, since I'm not alone in a cell now, I have company. That's generally supposed to be a favor here, but personally I felt happier in a cell on my own. However, it's not given to everyone to be like me, and feel perfectly well without other people, reading the good literature available here. For instance, at the moment I'm reading a journal called "Natur und Kultur," similar to "Kosmos" and "Umschau." ** I have the 1933 volume now, which even contains an account of Steinke's ultra rays, so you see, I can read about the most modern scientific findings here. Luckily I'm still in good health. It's very fortunate that I am naturally strong and was used to a simple life. I realize that by com-

---

* Swedish, "little wife."

† Italian, "little husband."

** The names of these journals translate as "Nature and Culture," "Cosmos," and "Survey."

paring myself with others.

At the end of 1937 Trude and Curt Teichert emigrate to Australia. But they keep up their correspondence with Ingeborg Magnusson. In the summer of 1938, Trude writes:

It's winter now, and I can assure you I've never been so cold! Winter here is like May at home, but the houses have no heating . . .

Some very good news: we've received the emigration permit for Rudolf, so now we must just hope that he gets out of there soon. The lawyer visited R. in June and writes:

"The general impression I had of him is good. He has been toughened up and made more resolute by the hard school he is going through. I don't think he has suffered mentally. Indeed, he has the serenity necessary to help him rise above outward difficulties. Physically he is perfectly all right. He is deeply tanned by working in the forest. His conduct is good, no one has ever complained of him. There is a possibility that he will be sent to what they call a moor camp (it is a kind of camp for doing community service). He is very pleased with this prospect. He has a chance to occupy his mind. There are many good books in the prison, including new ones, even some in his own field (for instance on the geology of Australia). He has learned shorthand and is studying English hard. Treatment is good. The Evangelical pastor in charge of censoring letters is particularly broad-minded."

16.7.38

Dear Father, you too are sure to have heard that the petition for clemency was turned down. I hadn't expected anything else, nor do I in the future. . . . At Liese's request, the Jewish prison teacher here recently talked to me about the possibility of emigration to Palestine. There wasn't much advice he could give me, particularly in view of my Evangelical faith, which of course I'm not giving up. . . . Whether I'd do better to go to Australia or Palestine I suppose can be decided only by whatever the circumstances are in a year's time. Personally I'd prefer Australia. I'm studying English regularly here so far as time allows. I don't let a day go by without reading a few pages. . . . Since June I've been working on building access roads to the Reich autobahn. It's really interesting, healthy work. And the construction company gives us 100 grams of sausage a day, and we can buy half a pound of butter substitute a week. Physically I'm feeling wonderful, as if I'd been training and were really fit, so I stand out because of that. . . . We're working in a beautiful part of the landscape, mainly in wooded areas. So far we've removed the topsoil with all its humus, using shovels, hoes, and carriers, and put it aside. It will be used later for growing turf beside the roads. From tomorrow on we'll probably be putting down gravel. I'll be a real Hercules by the time they let me out. I'm brown as a Negro down to the waist. Working in the open air is halfway to freedom.

11 September 1938

Dear Hans, dear Vera . . . Trude and Curt have managed to get me an emigration permit for Australia. Thank you for saying you'll have me to stay with you in London when I'm first released. So at least I'll know where to go in the first place, because Father has written to say that "for family reasons" I can't go to him as soon as I get out, but he hopes he can see me somewhere else. He also asked if there's some kind of institution, a home for newly released prisoners, where I could go until I leave for Australia. I tell myself that the reason why I'm not to go to Freiburg is that Else's relative "youthfulness"

and her "race" might officially be obstacles to my staying with
Father. I'll write myself in a week's time and ask him to explain what
he means more clearly. Perhaps you can find out something about all
this, without telling him that you already know about his explanation above. As for a "home," thank heaven there's no such thing!
These days no one's let out of here without being sent straight to a job
by the Labor Office. As I do brilliantly on the road-building work,
once I'm released there'd be nothing to stop me continuing to work for
a construction company until I emigrate, and so I'd be able to live
independently. I'm working hard to learn English. Unfortunately, I
really only get time for that on a Sunday. So I steal every minute I can
to keep it up. I've written something about Inge to Father too. I'm
afraid he was never particularly sympathetic to his children in
affairs of the heart.

As Father unfortunately—and for no real reason—thought that
he couldn't write to me to give me his opinion, could you write and
tell him it's not out of irresponsibility or any such thing that I want
to stay with my girl, and Inge too is ready to face an uncertain future
bravely. Hans, if you will write direct to me soon and answer this letter,
please tell me what Father thinks. I'm sure you are still in correspondence with Inge. So send her my heartfelt love, and encourage her too.

The Law for the Protection of German Blood and German
Honor contains a stipulation that Jews may not employ in their
households female citizens of German or related blood under
the age of 45. It is possible that Rudolf Kaufmann is thinking of
this paragraph when he suspects that his stepmother's "race"
and "youthfulness" are the reason why he will not be welcome
in Freiburg after his release from prison. His father seems to
feel that he and his second family are threatened more than

ever by the difficulties into which his son has fallen. He disapproves of Rudolf's Swedish connections, and in a formal note to Ingeborg Magnusson he expressly refuses to go on helping her and his son to correspond.

Freiburg, 3 Oct. 1938
    Dear Fräulein Magnusson,
My son Rudolf has requested me to forward you the enclosed letter, which I hereby do. I will ask you to turn for definite news of Rudolf only to his brother Hans in London, since in full awareness of my responsibility to Rudolf, to you, and to myself, I must unfortunately decline to forward further communications. With the greatest respect, I am yours . . .

In September 1938 Hans Kaufmann had already said, in a letter to Ingeborg Magnusson, that Rudolf was probably better off in prison than many of those at liberty in Germany, and in November, two weeks after "Kristallnacht,"* his wife Vera writes:

You know, harsh as it may sound, we are almost glad today to know that Rudolf is at least in prison under proper police guard, and not exposed to the despotic savagery of the Nazis. Countless prisoners have been taken in Germany recently, including old gentlemen over 80 years of age.—But now to happier subjects. We are really enjoying life in our new home. You must come and visit us soon to see the place . . .

At this period Inge must have been thinking of another journey, longer, more momentous and difficult and, if all went well, happier than a trip to London. She knows what Rudolf Kaufmann

---

* The notorious "Crystal Night" pogrom, which occurred during 9-10 November, 1938, so called because of the breaking of the windows of Jewish business premises, homes, and synagogues.

is planning to do on his release from prison. He intends to leave Germany, go to London, and then emigrate to Australia, and he will ask her to accompany him to a world that she knows as little as he does. He can't write and ask these difficult questions yet, but his sister Trude makes the points that Inge should bear in mind.

And now to another question, which I am afraid is indiscreet, but I hope I may ask it because we are such good friends: does R. have good reasons for writing to say that you will share his life here, or is it more like wishful thinking on his part in lonely hours? I don't want to comment before I know that. But if you are really contemplating it, good child that you are, then do think it over again and again! First, however, I will wait and see what you tell me. There will still be time for me to give you a clear idea of the opportunities and conditions in this country, for if you really intend to come you must know what you will be letting yourself in for. I am tormented by the thought that you could be torn away from a secure job, your family, and your native land, and find nothing here but problems and anxieties. It's bad enough for the lives of all the many Germans who have no choice in the matter to be ruined.

In March 1939 Rudolf Kaufmann is allowed to write a letter to Stockholm again for the first time in over two years. In fact, the prison administrative staff even encourage him to write. They are obviously keen on preparing the way early for Kaufmann to leave Germany as quickly as possible when he is released from custody.

So now I can write to you about what lies ahead of us, and the time which I hope we shall go through together hand in hand. . . . There's only half a year left keeping us apart, a time of anxious waiting. But that too will pass, and then it will be as if our years of separation had never been. We will pray to the Guide of all things that the world remains at peace for that length of time and longer, we'll pray that we can soon, soon see each other again. Ingelein, once we are together we MUST never part again, we will go through life together! That's my firm intention, and I know that my brave lille fru wants the same. It will make no difference even if our nearest and dearest are against it. Outward circumstances must not separate us any more. We must count on years, on decades together. Perhaps all our dear ones will have to fend for themselves without possessions some day, like the two of us now, relying again and again solely on their hands and their heads, their true support for each other and help from above. Times will be hard for all of us, no one will be able to trust in material goods. But we will have a much better substitute in ourselves. Ingelein, I did something bad to you back then, but today I'd like to tell you something to cheer you, something that was true in spite of everything! I was never unfaithful to you in my mind! And that's not all, no; before our Christmas in 1936 Herr and Frau Hirsch's daughter was in love with me, there was nothing I could do about it. My colleagues advised me to make what they called that "good match," and her parents would have liked it. Ingelein, I never wavered, for I knew what I had in you, and then I would have lost it for ever. I didn't want to tell you about this at the time. But today I think you'd like to hear about it, and I know that as my understanding moglie you will take it in the right spirit.—If everything goes well, as I and all of us hope, I will go straight to Hans on 12.10. My passport has been returned to me recently. I am so glad that Hans and Vera are kindly taking me in when I am first released. And if I go on *to Australia, then come what may I will take you with me. That must be our firm decision, even if our families may not understand it. . . . Ingelein, please do all you can to make it possible for you to emigrate to Australia too, if it comes to that! And write to tell Trude and Hans. Of course when you answer this letter you can reply to everything in it at length, saying what you think will be important to us in the future. I send you my love, consider yourself bacciata* with all my heart, and greetings to all our dear ones! Your lilleman Rudolf. P.S. Just the address as on the envelope will do.*

But all their plans come to nothing. All difficult decisions must be indefinitely postponed when the Wehrmacht invades Poland on 1 September 1939. Two days later Great Britain and France declare war on Germany. Travel between those countries is now impossible, financial transactions come to a standstill, even letters no longer cross the English Channel. If the letter that Kaufmann writes on 3 September ever reached England, then it went a long way round, probably by way of neutral Sweden.

Dear Hans and Vera, dear Inge. Thank you with all my heart for your letters. In spite of everything, let's not entirely give up hope that I can join you after my release. Even if the circumstances mean that I have to stay here in Germany, don't worry about me. I've been taking this other possibility into account for a year now, and if you reread the letter I wrote you a few months back, dear Inge, you may perhaps see that what then struck you as "optimism" was really well-founded pessimism. It was my fear that purely material complications in the outside world would separate us for years, even if I'd been able to travel from here to Australia. Yet again we see that our

---

* kissed.

fate, the fate of all of us, does not lie in human hands. We must accept that and hope. If we do see each other again in a few weeks' time after all, we'll regard it not as something we expected but as a very special gift of Providence. . . . Goodbye, and please cross your fingers, everyone, and hope I am released. Happy days to you, with heartfelt greetings from Rudolf!

Kaufmann is released punctually on 12 October 1939, just as the court specified in his sentence a little less than three years before, yet only because of a mistake on the part of the authorities. By now Jews who are not about to emigrate immediately are not set free after completing a prison sentence, but go to a camp—and Kaufmann can't emigrate. The war has barred his way. However, his visa for Australia is still helpful. It won't get him out of the country, but it saves him from the camp. In spring, when the permit was granted, the Coburg police had sent his passport to Amberg prison to speed up his emigration process on his release, and now no one notices that the prerequisites for anyone to travel abroad, Jews included, have entirely changed since then. Kaufmann is given his passport, is not even obliged to report regularly to the police, and can go anywhere he likes in Germany. As his father does not want him in Freiburg, he opts for Cologne, where his eldest brother and his brother's wife live. Of all the grown-up siblings, Albert is the only one who has not yet emigrated. Rudolf Kaufmann stays with him for a few days, resting. Even in wartime he can send letters to Sweden, which the German post office regards as a friendly country, and on 14 October he does indeed write a fifteen-page letter.

Rudolf Kaufmann, fall 1939

Yes, it's not a dream, I am really here with my brother Albert, all the official nonsense has been dealt with, and I can pour out my heart to my Ingelein, I can tell her all that's been on my mind so long.

His brother Hans, in a letter to Ingeborg Magnusson, once described Rudolf as a man skilled in the art of living, able to get something out of even the worst situations. Rudolf Kaufmann is still spurred on by his powers of optimism. The idea he uses to try fending off the approach of desperation is this: he and Inge are

chosen by fate to live not the lives of ordinary people, but of enlightened beings who have been tried and tested. Suffering and deprivation are their dear teachers. . . .

His belief in *the all-embracing, Divine Being who loves mankind*, he writes, has deepened in the last three years. He wants to talk to Inge about such things now, about everything that weighs on the mind—not forgetting what weighs on the body too. Imprisonment left him no choice but to be faithful to Inge. In this, he suspects, she must have had a harder time than he has endured these last few years. The love between him and her won't survive without physical closeness forever. So if, against all expectation, he can go to Australia, she must take the fateful step of leaving Sweden and following him. And if not, then she must try to make the great sacrifice of coming to Germany.

Not at once. No, I must find out if circumstances make it possible. There's a great demand for people to work here, and with all your skills it's certain that you could get a job anywhere. I must find out about all the other questions here first, nationality and so forth. If it can't be done, at least you must visit me. And time is pressing! I can't say why in so many words. You'll have to guess.

In the next few days and weeks Rudolf Kaufmann does not repeat this invitation, made two days after the end of a restricted but not dangerous three years spent behind prison walls. Rather, each of the long letters he writes to Stockholm in the time that follows withdraws it, without actually saying so. For those letters do not merely suggest but make it very clear that Germany is no longer a country where he and she could live together. There may still be places devoid of other human beings here and there, but they are out of Kaufmann's reach. He goes to Düsseldorf to do

what all of us in the same situation here do, work building roads. I'd heard that this is a good place for it, with many older workers, and the younger ones look after them very well. Many people have had to learn a new trade, and I'll find it useful to have spent a year and a half already on what they're only now learning to do. There are about 150 Js. here.

He is not seriously going to invite Inge into a country where he can no longer go out after eight in the evening, where he, a qualified geologist, is forbidden to continue working as a construction laborer after three days in the job, *because all the companies want to be rid of us*, a country where, within a few days of his newfound freedom, he feels he is under such pressure that he has to send cries for help with every letter.

And if you don't mind my asking, please send me a "package of love-gifts" now and then, I've found out that's allowed, and it can weigh up to 5 kilos. You're allowed to send: coffee, tea, butter, hardboiled eggs, crispbread, ham, chocolate, etc. Ingelein, you mustn't think my love for you is cupboard love, although there's a little truth in that proverbial saying . . .

Try to see if anything can be done in Sweden again . . . try visiting Professor Hede, Prof. Stensiö, Sven Hedin. You have my published work. There seem to be so few prospects. We must leave no stone unturned. Perhaps I could get a permit to stay in Sweden after all. . . .

Luckily my clothes are in reasonable order. I could do with a pullover, though. I half suspect that my Ingelein has a Christmas present ready for me. And Inge, I'd be very glad to have 2 or 3 pairs of thick woolly socks for work. My ski boots, new in 1937, will make good winter shoes. . . .

Kaufmann stays in Düsseldorf for three weeks. He finds a room with a Jewish married couple who give him a friendly welcome—for seventy of the hundred and five Reichsmarks he is to earn on the roads. The price includes lunch but not breakfast and supper. A young woman of his own age works for the Kochmanns, learning how to keep house. He talks to her a lot, goes for walks with her, they become friends. Kaufmann's attitude to her resembles Inge's, a little while ago, with a young man in Sweden.

You write that you were "nearly unfaithful to me." Ingelein, I know that you couldn't and didn't really do it, even if it would have been the right sort of "unfaithfulness" in the eyes of society. You have the inner will for that, you are convinced that we alone belong together, in spite of everything. . . .

I know that this girl Margot is in love with me. But I told her at once that you are all I have, that I could never live for anyone but you. She saw that at once. . . .

So today I thought I'd write to you at once and ask you to accept poor Margot into our circle of friends. . . . Ingelein, I've been able to look very deep into many human souls in the last 3½ years. So I am not ashamed of my own human soul and its temptations and needs any more. And neither must you be. I will always try to put my whole soul into the lines that I write you, for just now, and perhaps for a long time of trial yet to come, that's all we can give each other. You will be able to read so much between the lines, just as I do in your letters.

Kaufmann cannot stay on in Düsseldorf. If he were a resident of the city, he would at best be employed in civil engineering there. As he isn't, he is supposed to go to Coburg where he comes from, or back to Königsberg where he also comes from, or somewhere else, anywhere.

Ingelein, can't you summon up the courage to go to the King with recommendations from Stensiö and Hedin? We have to try everything! I also expect that I may be sent to Lublin in Poland. All I want to do is work and earn a living.

Word has quickly spread that the Reich Railroad company has recently started operating special trains of a new kind. The first of these trains ran from Austria and Moravia to Poland on 12 October, the day of Kaufmann's release from prison.

Cologne, 9.11.39

Dear Ingelein,
I was so pleased to get your sweet letter, and of course very pleased with the "package of love-gifts" too. It [arrived] intact and unin-

jured, which isn't always the case. . . . Just think, I'm off to Kbg. to see Wolfgang and Benno. That's to say, Wolfgang is still away fighting, but his family live there. I can't work here, but there I have a job and a permit. I hope nothing will happen to spoil it. If the general call-up takes me to Poland, I'll accept that "like a man" too. You know I can be brave. And I'm through with the other thing. There were only a few pangs of a certain kind afterwards. I have spent a couple of pleasant afternoons and evenings in harmony and friendship with Margot and her sister. . . . How do I spend my evenings, you ask? In D. it was almost always with my kind landlord and landlady. I hardly had a chance to write. And when I'm alone? With my beloved trilobites—now you really ought to be jealous of those. I may meet Jim in Berlin. . . . Once I'm working in Kbg. then I'll write you a loving letter from my heart again. But I must get into a more collected frame of mind first. You'll understand. Recently I was reading The Odyssey, Ingelein. When it came to Odysseus and Calypso and Circe, and he was still longing for Penelope, I couldn't help feeling as if so much of it was written with me in mind.

I'll close now, Ingelein. I'm in such haste. I love you so much. I can say so now.

In the middle of November 1939, Rudolf Kaufmann returns to Königsberg by way of Berlin. But he cannot just stay there.

It's been suggested to me that if I don't emigrate I'll have to go back to my old place of work or somewhere similar.

Inge, too, must have wondered what he meant. Prison? A camp? A ghetto? The firm of Orient-Palestine-Lloyd, No. 2 Meinecke Str. Berlin, could get him a passage to Chile. It would cost two hundred dollars, money that Kaufmann does not have, that Inge in Stockholm does not have, that his brother Hans can't send from London because of the wartime currency restrictions, money that the aid committees could give with as much justification to thousands, ten of thousands of others in equally dangerous situations. In Königsberg, Kaufmann finally strikes out on his own behalf. From mid-December, the letters he sends to Stockholm have Lithuanian stamps on them and are postmarked Kaunas. It is a few weeks before he ventures to hint at the way he arrived there.

I have a very adventurous time behind me, and now at least I can lift the veil a little and say a few brief words. Came here under cover of night and fog, with the aid of good money and good words. Had to stay anonymous. Once escaped being sent back only by chance. Running and running all the time. Tried again and again to make connections. Threatened with transport back, attempt to get away at station. Was beaten up. Phone call back at last minute. Unexpected connections in extraordinary context. Three days' grace. Had to disappear somehow or other. Now: a visa to stay and prospects of temporary post as geologist. These latest ups and downs, plus 2 days under arrest, less than a week ago. If I described it all in detail it would sound like some incredible novel. You'll understand that I can only hint at all this. But now, for the time being, everything's all right. And I know that when you read this you too will have a great fright at first, and then feel even greater joy. I've always lived a long way off, never been settled. You'll understand. But now it's all right. The Jews here have treated me so well, it's touching. And I'm getting a little support from a large organization. Now I hope I can have my clothes etc. sent on to me. . . .

At first Kaufmann dared not even write back to Germany under his own name. He just sent packets of butter anonymously to Margot, the Kochmanns, and his brother in Cologne, labeled "Sample, no commercial value": nourishing greetings with no sender's name, but no doubt the recipients were able to interpret what they meant.

In Kaunas he finds accommodation with a family of German-Jewish origin who run a bookshop selling French, German, and English literature, Pribačis, at No. 48 Laisvės alėja. He cannot pay rent. Instead, he helps out in the shop now and then, and for the rest he depends on the Holzmans' friendship. When the family has gone to bed he sleeps on the sofa in the living room.

It's all very well to keep telling myself: "There's no alternative, I can't do anything about it at the moment." But it's so dismal and difficult, having to live at other people's expense.

Kaunas is overflowing with fugitives, particularly from occupied Poland. So far Lithuania, like Sweden, has been spared the war. But there are fears in both countries that this state of affairs might change overnight.

For the time being we must be glad we're alive at all, don't you think? … People here have been badly affected by the general turmoil. That's only too easy to understand. Whose turn will it be today? Whose turn tomorrow? I keep trying to be brave, although it's been seven years now and I still can't reach my goal. . . .

Every day I realize how lucky I was to find the courage to get out of Germany in time. You hear cries of distress everywhere from Germans who arrive in Lublin as beggars. And what would have happened to me!?! I'm afraid there's no legal way of helping anyone any more. There are about 30,000 refugees or more here now. I'm "little brother" to everyone here at the Holzmans' now, and I think of the two girls, one of them is 15 and the other is 17 years old, as my sisters. They're such nice, educated, sensitive people, they'd fit in really well with our own friends.

When he fled to Kaunas, Rudolf Kaufmann had to leave not only his clothes but also his photos of Inge behind, and probably her letters too. Now he asks her to send him a new photograph of herself—particularly the one of her *sketching on Skansen*, and others too if possible.

It is now four years since they last saw each other, and almost every day brings news that moves the prospect of a meeting further away. The Lithuanian postal charges are some slight comfort.

It's so nice that letters to you go at the inland rate. It gives me a kind of feeling that somehow or other we've come closer to each other.

I won't say much about Kaunas, the country, the people, and so on: in different times, all that would have been interesting. But I can't write as I'd like to, and I prefer to touch only on what concerns you and me. To outward appearance, though, I'm in the thick of things here. I take the time to go skating, I borrowed skates somewhere, I sometimes go to a café too, I've been out dancing with people in my own situation, I get invitations. I sometimes have to put on a bit of a show, I make contacts, I eat, I drink, I sleep, somehow the whole day is so full that I hardly get time to think, read, and write. And yet in a way that's just my outer self. I can't express what I mean properly, but I'm sure you will understand. Somehow at this time, when every day brings something different, when coincidence follows hard on the heels of coincidence, I feel that fundamentally I'm not my own master any more, I'm somehow being guided by "Fate." I take action as best I can, yet I'm dependent on fate. And I'm probably not the only one to feel like this.

In Lithuania, Kaufmann sees more than ever before of what he calls "real Judaism."

Photograph on postcard, Kaunas 11.4.1940. " . . . Here you see me with a nice man, a companion in the same situation. Like me, he wants to go to Haiti. Ask if there's a Haitian consulate where you are."
Rudolf Kaufmann on the sofa in the Holzman family's living room.

I hope I can soon go to Vilnius. Vilnius is an interesting old city and these days a positive Babel of nations. There's still a real ghetto there with its ancient customs and traditions, a place that hasn't by any means been really discovered. Herr Holzman is going to show me everything.

Old Jewish culture arouses his curiosity—the kind of curiosity that a traveler feels when, at the same time, he is ill at ease in unfamiliar surroundings.

I'm afraid I don't feel really Jewish inside. There's so much heartfelt love among them, but they have so little freedom of thought and action, fettered as they are by ancient traditions and prejudices, and isolated from the world. Yiddish folk songs are beautiful . . .

From Australia, Kaufmann receives a final rejection of his application to emigrate. But his brother sends a telegram from London: "Permit Chile certain must wait two or three months." The way to Chile is via Haiti, and Stockholm could be a stopping-off point on the way to the Caribbean. But is there a Haitian consulate in Stockholm? And it is not clear exactly what Hans is doing in London to ease the way for his brother's emigration overseas. Apparently a kind of poll tax is levied on every refugee who is leaving. Hans is willing to pay it, but in the end it all comes to nothing. It turns out that Hans has been taken in by a swindler, and gave him a good deal of money in return for nonexistent travel opportunities. He spares his brother in Kaunas the precise details.

If the times were less turbulent, Kaufmann could probably work as a geologist in Lithuania. Colleagues at the Geological Institute of the University are interested in getting him to collaborate with them. He spends hours of unpaid work at the Institute preparing fossil placoderms from northern Lithuania, hoping for a post later, and he writes a paper on trilobites for a geologists' conference without knowing if he will get permission to deliver it. No work permits are being granted to any emigrants in Lithuania at this time. But after the end of March 1940, Kaufmann works as a supervisor in the dining room of a Jewish primary school between twelve and three in the afternoon, five days a week, getting a free meal and 60 litas a month. It's a start.

It seems to us all a miracle that we can still buy and own things freely here. We none of us like to think of the distant future. We don't want to think too much of our own fate either, let alone the hopes we all cherish. "Getting by together"—that depends so much on work permits, residence permits, visas, transit visas, religion, race, class, nationality, credentials, travel connections, contacts, on luck and chance, on hard toil and going the rounds. What's going to happen now? A long war? Some kind of revolution? Ingelein, fate is so hard and words of comfort so empty. I was so happy when you wrote saying that you had always felt so peaceful and safe with me. Ingelein, it would all be the same again at once, if only I had a little firm ground under my feet, proper work, a paid job, my own earnings. Luckily I'm with such nice people here, they've taken me in like their own son, I'm their "little brother" (the word's "broliukas" in Lithuanian). And yet I can't shake off the miserable feeling that I'm only a burden on others. When I'm working at the University I don't know if there's any point in that either, if I'll be able to finish my work, whether I can ever have the prospect of a post. I don't hang my head, in spite of the seven hard years behind me and however many there may be still ahead. Yet I'd so much like to be with you. Then we could both pour out our hearts and tell each other all our troubles.

In April 1940, German troops occupy Denmark and Norway. In May they overrun Holland, Luxembourg, and Belgium. In the middle of June Paris falls to them without a fight. Once again, Rudolf Kaufmann urges Ingeborg Magnusson to join him. At least for a visit. Better still, to stay. He understands her hesitation in view of the uncertain, unpredictable situation all over the world—any country, even Lithuania, even Sweden, can be drawn into the war overnight—but then again he doesn't quite understand it either. For if there's danger everywhere, then Inge might just as well wait for more peaceful times at his side.

All these years of separation are not a small thing for either of us. At least make what preparations you can for a possible journey. You can always make the final decision when the moment comes. Because I'm afraid that the situation isn't going to let us meet for the next few months.

A week after receiving this letter, Inge will be able to read newspaper reports that the Red Army has occupied the whole of Lithuania. The Russians had taken over some individual bases as early as 1939, when the Baltic states were allotted to the Soviet sphere of influence in the secret additional clause to the pact between Hitler and Stalin. On 16 June, a day after the invasion, Kaufmann repeats his invitation to Inge—in a tone of urgency that he has never used before.

Reinhard Kaiser

Be that as it may, I don't think it's particularly dangerous to come here, no more dangerous than in other situations at this difficult time. There's been a period of turbulence here too, but things are calming down. However, even in times of turmoil you'd always be safe and have the chance to go home, being a neutral foreigner. I think it's so important in our own interests for us to see each other again now. . . . It's not entirely out of the question that I'll be able to work permanently in the country of our eastern neighbors some time, indeed that I'll have to. And then, Ingelein, you would be faced with a very big decision over joining me. I'm sometimes afraid and sick at heart when I think that, if that happened, you'd be exchanging a safer job and more peaceful life for a prole-tarian existence and little prospect of ever seeing your native land again, all because of me. . . . As soon as I get a permit to live and work in some country, any country, we must be together, that is if we really ever want that, if we ever can be together. If not, it would be better for us to say "Goodbye" now. The events of the last few days have shown me all this so clearly. These are pitiless times and call for such hard decisions: for or against. What I'm asking you, darling, is to be entirely, actively prepared for the hard times that no human being in any part of the earth will be spared. Do you think that Hans and Vera, Curt and Trude, anyone at all will be safe from them? Do you think that your own country might not pass laws some time forbidding us to marry? Ingelein, you must think hard about all this. I wish everything could be quite differ-ent. But we mustn't pursue unlikely mirages of hope any more and forget what the present is like. . . . These difficult times are only just beginning and will last many, many years, perhaps until we die. If we don't find our way to each other soon we may not have another chance. We're both older now, and if we're ever to think of family happiness it must be soon. At our age, we mustn't keep pursuing vague dreams. Ingelein, I have written harshly today, and inside I want to be so tender. It's the hard times that make me write like this, and the roar of tanks rumbling by, and the pitiless humming of squadrons of aircraft flying past. It's war, for us too, and we are faced with great decisions. Look, dear Ingelein, we really must make our minds up, for one thing because it's very hard to live all alone, and full freedom for me to be with other women and for you to be with other men would raise great emotional problems. Here again it's so hard, especially in such sad times, when you're alone and you want help from others. Ingelein, I still think of you so much. I am asking a great deal of you. Yet I must do it, I see no way out. I kiss you with all my heart, and am your lilleman, Rudolf.

The situation of the refugees in Kaunas is no less secure after the Red Army's invasion, indeed quite the opposite. The mighty Soviet Union will be in a better position than little Lithuania to halt the unpredictable German war plans. But disquiet is abroad everywhere. No one knows what will happen next. The Holzmans, Kaufmann's hosts, have been in despair since hearing that their bookshop is to be closed. Once again Kaufmann hopes for a permanent appointment as a geologist, but he could equally well be sent to Siberia to work on the roads, or to the Urals as a miner. At this moment of political crisis his love swings between dream and despair. His dramatic appeal for them to begin their life together at what appears to be the last possible moment is followed, two weeks later, by a fall into the hopeless void and a second farewell.

Reinhard Kaiser

I am so sick at heart today. And I feel so little courage to face our future together. We have both had very bad luck, and I don't know how it will all turn out. You see, several things have happened that destroy all my hopes. This country, Ingelein, faces great changes. And if I were to get a firm footing here I'd have to say no to everything else for ever. There are upheavals ahead in society and politics such as we can't even imagine. . . . I'd like to spare you and myself a future full of anxiety if there's any other possibility. I don't feel at all strong and brave any more, even in my love for you. I know how hard it must be for you when I write such things. But I can't tell lies. The short time we have spent together, our long separation, the anxieties of the last few months and every moment now, the hopeless prospects for the future—they are all to blame. . . . Yes, fate is so bitter for us both, Ingelein, and after all this it's probably better for us to give up our hopes of each other. . . . Try to be free, as free as you can. There's too little hope of our meeting for any length of time in the foreseeable future. . . . Wouldn't it be better if we didn't cling so closely together, then we wouldn't have to torment ourselves so much? Perhaps you can forget me with another man. . . . I am hurting you so much, and it is such a bitter disappointment for you. Perhaps there may yet be some way out. I take you in my arms again and kiss you with all my heart. Your lilleman Rudolf.

Their hope of living together has been maintained and nourished by letters alone for four years. In July 1940 it crumbles. The old optimism on which Kaufmann could draw in what at times was almost incredible abundance has run out. Love at a distance has become harder and harder for him since his release from prison nine months ago. In July 1940 he gives up. But the link does not break. Letters still pass between them, if not so often. Only his, as already mentioned, have been preserved. In them he speaks of a life in exile into which, unexpectedly, a kind of peace returns.

For the last time, Rudolf Kaufmann has a strange stroke of luck amidst his misfortunes. A month after the proclamation of the Lithuanian Socialist Soviet Republic, he is given a permanent appointment as a qualified geologist, with a regular salary.

It is five-thirty in the afternoon, Moscow time, and my day's work is finished. After so many years I'm a geologist again, working with my rocks. I still don't know how long it will last, but that doesn't matter at the moment. I'm working again, and that's enough for now. I sit all day by a beautiful river bank in the forest, no one comes here, just me and my assistants and friends Vitas and Petrukas, two farmers' boys who take turns washing rocks in a sieve in the river for me—the rocks come from the debris of the marl walls. Otherwise it's all nature, just water, wind, sun, trees, air, grasses, flies, peace, and rocks. I'm living in the hayshed. I've put my bed in there and I can forget the hurry and bustle of town life for a while. . . . At the moment I have found a little peace again here, working in natural surroundings, and I think of you. . . . It's so terribly sad that this uncertainty has destroyed our hopes. And yet it was right for us not to feel bound to each other any more. We all have such a horror of what tomorrow may bring, we have to force ourselves not to think of it too much. I see, with the Holzmans and others, how fast we move from the heights to the depths, and how no one is spared. I have no idea yet whether I'll be staying in Lithuania. I don't know what the situation will be about my nationality either. Perhaps I can or should become a Lithuanian citizen. I don't know yet. I just hope that they can do with me as a geologist. That's my only chance. Would you have been able to get a permit to visit? Ingelein, sometimes I'd so much like to take a great leap and be with you. But I have an injured knee and must stay here. Ingelein, I hope you will find some kind of small happiness there without me. I'll probably have to wait far too long for anything like that.

It's a pity you can't be here with me, helping me to count rocks. I am still sleeping in the hay, washing at the spring, living on milk, eggs, and butter, and in my work I can forget all the world events going on around us. It could be so beautiful but for the great anxieties that we all feel in more or less the same way. . . .

So now I'm sitting at the table in the farmhouse living room, there are people here, they're rather merry, I don't understand a word of it, I'm listening with only half an ear because I'm thinking of you. Dear Ingelein, I thank you from my heart for all your love, and I am so sad that it can't be fulfilled. . . .

My knee is nicely healed now. Luckily there were no great after-effects of this second accident of mine. Of course I must go carefully. . . . I have to thank the doctor who has been treating me unpaid so far. I hope I can pay it all back to him. In fact I'm beginning to, although he protested, and I'm starting to pay back the Holzmans too. I have a companion in misfortune, a nice man, who rents out little rooms. And there's another, larger room which is rented. The landlord and landlady occupy the two living rooms. Everyone here has a right to 9 m² living space, which is a good deal. I really do hope you will have a little room of your own some time. I feel for you so much, it's so hard always having to think of others and never have a chance to be on your own, or alone with people you love, or with the person you love best. Ingefru, it's dark now. I'm already looking forward to your next letter. . . .

This fall there are fewer letters from Lithuania to Sweden. Kaufmann sends one in October, one in November, and one in December. A new character appears in the October letter, a woman of his own age, Ilse, who has emigrated from Tilsit. Fate, he writes, brought them closer to each other. And in November he is speaking of their coming marriage. Kaufmann thinks he owes Inge in Stockholm an account of the details, or believes that it is reasonable for him to send them: his first salary as a permanently appointed government geologist, he says, together with Ilse's savings, were enough for two dresses and a pony-skin coat, and now they can start thinking of furniture and linen. He knows, he writes, that he will hurt Inge by speaking of his new happiness. But he also knows that she can be glad of it, as one woman to another. In December he writes that he loves Ilse and she loves him, but she'll probably never be such a good walking companion as Inge would have been. That will hardly have been much of a comfort to Inge. She is left waiting in vain for post from Lithuania in January and February. Not until March does he reply to two letters from her—

. . . one a little reproachful, but so sweet, and then the other, the last one.

I know how sad my meeting Ilse must have made you. Believe me, it was hard for me to give up the hope of being with you too. I hadn't known Ilse long last summer when everything changed, but we didn't really come to know and love each other until much later, long after there was any prospect that you and I could live together. Ingelein, you can't imagine how hard life is here too, and how hard it will be, and I have known many hours when I simply thought I was too weak to go on living. Everything is very difficult for me even now. I have the burden of very responsible work on my shoulders. I spent two months here on geological surveys, cut off from Kaunas. The post sleigh takes 17 hours, and we worked until midnight every day. And the work is far from done even now. Above all, this kind of work is so strange to me, there's my difficulty with the language, the limited financial means. But there are 40–80 men working under me. Ingelein, believe me, back in the fall when I met Ilse I had so many anxieties, and that was why fate brought us together so quickly. We both needed help from each other, outwardly and inwardly. Ingelein, if fate had brought you here by force, which is what happened to us emigrants, nothing would ever have parted us. But as things are it has turned out for the best. For we don't know what tomorrow and the day after will bring.

The last letter that Rudolf Kaufmann sends to Ingeborg Magnusson in Stockholm is the first to be written on a typewriter—clumsily, with all kinds of mistakes, and ignoring the rule that you add a space after commas and full stops.

Dr. R. Kaufmann
Kaunas. Prusu g. 10a   *Skirsnemune, 23.4.41*

Dear Ingelein
Thank you for your last sweet letter. I hope you are quite better again. When people are exhausted and sick they lose all their relish for life, and I know that at heart you have a great deal of joie

de vivre. Wait for spring and summer. Then everything may well look different. Ingelein, since I last wrote about a month ago Ilse and I have married. We are very happy together, although we have spent hardly 5 days with each other in all this time. I am almost always out doing work in the field. We don't have our own home yet either. My room is in Vilnius, Ilse's in Kaunas, and I am usually living somewhere completely different. We celebrated with just a few friends, but we thought of all our dear ones elsewhere. I have at last had more detailed news about Hans, through Liese. She writes that he was interned last summer,* but not for long, and is back in his old job again now. Of course I was very glad to hear it. In January I inquired at the Red Cross for Hans's whereabouts, and had a telegram from Hans himself soon before the arrival [of] Liese's letter, saying that he and Vera were well. Liese is the happy mother of a sturdy boy now, and is naturally very proud of him. She has heard from Curt and Trude that everything is the same with them. I regularly get news from Albert and Helene. Thank you very much for the photographs from Bornholm. I would very much like, if possible, to go to Bornholm again, and Sweden, and see the trilobites. You know that we both liked them. Ingelein, it just couldn't turn out differently, it couldn't turn out the way we once imagined. Thank you so much for not grudging [us] our happiness. Believe me, we don't have an easy time here, no one can say so. The language, the surroundings, these times. My work is so full of responsibility too and so new to me. Ingelein, give my regards to Sweden, Skansen, Stockholm, and your family. With best regards from Ilse too

---

* When war was declared on Germany in 1939, many of the Germans and Austrians who had fled from the Nazis to Great Britain were interned for a while on the Isle of Man.

Dr: R.Kaufmann.
Kaunas.Prusu g.10a.   Skirsnemune. 23.4.41.

Liebes Ingelein,
Ich danke Dir sehr fuer Deinen lieben letzten Brief. Hoffentlich bist
Du auch wieder ganz gesund geworden.Wenn man abgehetzt und krank ist,
so vergeht einem ja ganz die Lebensfreude und ich weiss,dass Du doch
im Grunde lebensfreudig bist.Lass erst den Fruehlingund den Sommer
kommen.Dann mag alles wieder anders aussehen.Ingelein,inzwischen ,et-
wa vor einem Monat haben Ilse und ich geheiratet.Wir sind recht glueck-
lich miteinander,obgleich wir in dieser Zeit zusammengerechnet kaum 5
Tage beieinander waren.Ich bin ja fast immer im Gelaende taetig.Ein
Heim haben wir auch noch nicht.Mein Zimmer ist in Vilnius,das von Ilse
in Kaunas und leben tue ich meistens ganz woanders. Wir feierten nur mit ein
paar Freunden,dachten aber an alle unsre Lieben da draussen. Endlich habe ich durch Liese genauere Nachricht ueber Hans erhalten.Sie schreibt,
dass er im vorigen Sommer nur fuer kurze Zeit interniert war und jetzt
wieder in seiner alten Stellung taetig ist.Ich habe mich natuerlich sehr
darueber gefreut.Im Januar liess ich beim Roten Kreuz nach Hans'ens
Verbleib anfragen und erhielt kurz vor Erhalt Lieses Briefs von Hans
selber ein Telegramm,dass Vera und er "well" seien.Liese ist die glueck-
liche Mutter eines strammen Jungen geworden und ist natuerlich sehr
stolz darauf.Vor Kurt und Tude erfuhr sie,dass dort alles beim alten et
stehe.Von Albert und Helene erhalte ich regelmaessig Nachricht.Fuer die
Fotografieen aus Bornholm danke ich Dir noch sehr. Ich haette Lust,
wenn es ginge wieder nach Bornholm,nach Schweden und zu den Trilobiten
zu fahren.Du weisst ja,dass wir sie beide lieb hatten. Ing-lein,es ging
eben alles nicht anders und so,wie wir es uns einst vorgestellt hatten.
Ich danke Dir so sehr,dass Du unser Glueck hier goennst.Glaub mir,wir haben es hier nicht leicht,man kann das alles nicht so recht sagen. Die
Sprache,die Umgebung und die Zeit.Meine Arbeit ist ja auch so verantwor-
tungsvoll und so neu fuer mich. Ingelein,gruess mir Schweden,Skansen,
Stockholm und die Angehoerigen alle.Herzliche Gruesse auch von Ilse

Something was left out of this last letter. There is no signature.
The letterhead does contain the name of the sender—typed—but
in the place where his name will be really missed, where its
absence leaves a gap, there is nothing. Rudolf Kaufmann did
not sign his name to his last letter. It is something that can eas-

ily happen to the inexperienced typist. Before taking the typed sheet of paper out of the machine he is probably aware that there is still something to be added by hand. But the mechanical process of typing produces a deceptively perfect appearance, and when he has taken the paper out he feels as if turning the roller finished the job. The letter is folded. It is written only on one side. The characters disappear inside a double fold. And with them so does the empty space. An envelope lies ready to hand. The letter is put into it, the envelope is stuck up, provided with an address, taken to the post office, stamped, postmarked, sent off. Two days later the woman to whom the letter is written finds the gap at the end of it. However long she stares at the void after that other name—the name of the other woman, the name Ilse—the missing name she wants to see does not appear on the paper.

The letter from Skirsnemune is dated 23 April 1941. Two months later, on 22 June, the German assault on Russia begins. The attack by the Army Group North is aimed at Leningrad by way of the surroundings of Königsberg and Memel, then through Lithuania and the other Baltic states. SS Special Action groups and the Security Police, following hard on the heels of the regular army troops of the Wehrmacht, begin eliminating Jews, gypsies, and political commissars. There are no lists of the names of victims, only numbers. Those who carried out the operations calculated, recorded, and passed the details on themselves. Numbers mattered to them, names didn't.

The number for Lithuania is 136,421.

* * *

The box I had bought at auction that Saturday afternoon in May 1991 contained only letters with German stamps—the first postmarked in Georgenswalde in the Samland, then several sent from Königsberg, one from Marienburg (by way of a postal bus service to Danzig), most of them from Coburg, finally some from Cologne and Düsseldorf. The last of those letters was posted from Königsberg again on 27.11.1939: *Guess what—by the time you have this letter in your hands, I'll be tapping at ammonites in outcrops of rock! Yes, geology has me under its spell again, and in these hard times too! I'll write you a nice long letter soon. . . .*

An open-ended story.

I knew nothing about the real end.

I was almost sure, however, that Ingeborg Magnusson was no longer alive. The fact that the letters had surfaced in Frankfurt indicated as much. It was hard to imagine her simply giving them away herself. After her death, perhaps when her Stockholm apartment was cleared, they had probably ended up with a junk dealer who sent them for auction to Germany, where German letters and German stamps would fetch higher prices than in Sweden or other countries.

However, it was possible, if not probable, that Rudolf Kaufmann was still alive. At first, after I had begun reading his letters, I kept catching myself wondering if he in person might have been the invisible adversary who was bidding against me at the auction, going well above what (so far as I could judge) was any sensible philatelic limit. He would have had a motive—to rescue his own story, which was now lying in front of me and not him, making claims. Its main claim was not to be lost from view.

I began looking for clues to Rudolf Kaufmann.

Anyone who sometimes adds "Dr." to his name in the sender's details on envelopes has, one may assume, written a doctoral thesis. It wasn't difficult to find Rudolf Kaufmann's. It was more difficult for me even to begin to understand his "Study of the Statistics of Variation Through the Modification and Transformation of Species in the Upper Cambrian Trilobite Genus *Olenus* Dalm." But I was less interested in the details of his researches than in the fact that he had found his trilobites in an alum quarry at Andrarum in the southern Swedish region of Skåne, and the passage on page 12 of his dissertation where he describes the device he used to measure the subjects he was studying. "My father, Prof. W. Kaufmann of Königsberg, constructed one of these measuring instruments, and I would like to express my gratitude to him here." *Kürschner's Gelehrtenkalender** lists German professors quite fully, with their academic careers and most important publications, and the German *Who's Who* of 1935 even gave me Walter Kaufmann's family details: "Married I) Berlin, 1900, Frieda Kuttner, d. 1928; II) Berlin, 1932, Else Bath. Children: 4 sons, 2 daughters."

It was more surprising to find the name Rudolf Kaufmann again in a different kind of list of scholars, giving the names of German scientific researchers now without appointments and published in London in 1936 by the "Emergency Community of German Scientists Abroad." In this list, where he appears to have been even more of a polyglot than I had

* Kürschner's Calendar of Scholars.

gathered from his letters, he features as: "KAUFMANN, Dr. Rudolf, researcher; born 1909, single. (English, French, Italian, Spanish, Danish, Norwegian, Swedish.) 1932/33: researcher, Geological-Paleontological Institute, Greifswald University; 1933: researcher, Copenhagen University; 1934: researcher, Istituto di Geologia, Bologna University. SPEC [iality]: paleontology; microtectonics; ontogeny. Unpl[aced]."

Also surprising was my discovery—in the "Germany Reports" published by the Prague Committee in Exile of the Social Democratic Party, which regularly contained long lists of the verdicts in cases brought for offences against the racial laws—of the mention in December 1936 of Rudolf Kaufmann's case, although without his name: "Coburg Criminal Court: a 27-year-old Jew to 3 years in prison."

But as for Andrarum, where Rudolf Kaufmann had worked and done his research—I couldn't find it anywhere on the maps of Sweden that I studied.

Not until a year later, in the summer of 1992 as my family and I were driving north from Trelleborg along the Baltic coast of Sweden and passed a road junction, did I see a signpost to "Andrarum 7 km." I did not turn off. We were due to drive four hundred kilometers further north that day to take delivery of a key to the holiday house we had rented. But two weeks later, driving back to Germany, we did take a detour inland— without high hopes of finding the quarry by ourselves in that densely forested area. However, signs led us to "Andrarums Alunbruk," the Andrarum Alum Quarry, which had been made into an open-air museum and industrial monument, with information boards, a kiosk, and footpaths. On a scree slope below a steep, quarried wall my daughter found a fossilized trilobite.

I had not had any difficulty in persuading my family to take our summer vacation in Sweden. I wanted to see the street in Stockholm where Ingeborg Magnusson had lived, to find out

The alum quarry in Andrarum

whether the building still stood, and what it looked like. We drove from our holiday house on the Skara coast to spend a day in Stockholm. I found the street, I found the building, a large, renovated apartment block dating from the turn of the twentieth century. I photographed it as well as I could from the other side of the street. Finally I crossed to glance at the set of doorbells, and there, among the other names, I found the name of—Magnusson.

I was astonished, although it is not exactly an unusual name in Sweden, and it was quite possible that the Magnussons who now lived in the Skeppargatan building had nothing to do with Ingeborg Magnusson. I did not ring the bell that summer of 1992, one reason being that I don't speak Swedish. But I also feared to appear suddenly as an unauthorized intruder on a stranger's private property. Only months later, and with the help of a translator colleague who does know Swedish, did I write a letter to "Herr och fru Magnusson" at that address. It reached Ingeborg's now very elderly sister, who was still living in their old apartment.

Greta Magnusson, it turned out, had many further letters written by Rudolf Kaufmann to her sister—more than I already had in my possession. These letters, which she sent me together with some photographs, complemented and completed the story. Some were from the time of the young couple's meeting in Bologna, but most dated from Kaufmann's stay in Lithuania. There were also letters to Ingeborg from Kaufmann's brother and sister, Hans Kaufmann and Trude Teichert. I learned from Greta Magnusson what I had not known before: that the star-crossed lovers never met again. That the Germans had killed Rudolf Kaufmann. He had married another woman, Ilse, a few months before the Wehrmacht invaded Lithuania. And that Ingeborg Magnusson never married, and died in 1972.

Stockholm, Skeppargatan 66

The story was not open-ended any more. That made it no easi-er for me to decide what to do with it. Ever since the first letters came into my hands I had been trying to sketch out a novel based on them. All my attempts failed, and I now think I know why. I could add nothing to a story that I could not have made up in the form in which I found it; I could only distort or damage it.

Everything that I invented to make the incidents more vivid and graphic, to close or bridge the gaps in the record, was obviously a minor ingredient and showed that it was added later—particularly the dialogue. There was another obstacle too. With a story that I want to turn into a novel, I feel that I have to be able to play about with it in certain ways. But I found that I could not play with this one, and I was less and less able to do so the more I immersed myself in it. As a way out of this blind alley, I thought of writing a radio program. In the restricted space of sixty minutes or thirty-two manuscript pages, I would give some account of the material, of what I knew about the real story.

Now I could no longer postpone the long overdue visit to Coburg, where Rudolf Kaufmann had worked as a teacher, where Inge Magnusson had visited him at the end of 1935, and where the police had arrested him in early August 1936. The trial and indeed Kaufmann's arrest had, as I expected, left plenty of traces behind them in the local press. The Coburg archivist also showed me files about the Preacher Hirsch boarding school, among them Rudolf Kaufmann's job applications, and he told me the way to the Hohe Strasse above the town center of Coburg, where the villa in which the school was housed still stands.

The radio manuscript became a sketch for something larger. A combination of narrative and quotation seemed to provide a workable model, and the writing came easily to me. The first version of the book was ready at the beginning of December 1995, and the publisher had already approved it, when the whole project, which had arisen in the first place from chance and my luck in finding the letters and had just taken distinct form, had to be changed again in the light of more unhoped-for finds.

In a book that I saw only because my wife, who had read the proofs, was sent a printed copy, I found a chapter about Kaunas containing a description of the Laisvės alėja. This was the street where the Pribačis bookshop had stood, the place where Rudolf Kaufmann took refuge after his flight from Germany. The bookshop itself is also mentioned in Verena Dohrn's book *Baltische Reise*,* and in her description of old Kaunas the author refers to the daughter of the former bookseller, Margarete Holzman, now living in Giessen. I realized at once that I had already read about her—in the account given by Rudolf Kaufmann, whose letters to Stockholm mention the two daughters of Holzman the bookseller, one aged fifteen and the other seventeen at the time. I found Margarete Holzman's number in the Giessen telephone book. "I believe," I said, when I had introduced myself, "that you knew someone whose story I have been tracing for the last five years, Rudolf Kaufmann." "Oh, Rudi!" she cried. "How good to find someone taking an interest in his sad fate!"

Margaret Holzman told me a great deal about Kaunas and the emigrants who came to her parents' house. She immediately recognized the "nice man, the companion in the same situation" with whom Rudolf Kaufmann is shown making plans for traveling to Haiti in one of the pictures that I had been sent from Stockholm. "That's Herr Löw." "And where are the two of them sitting?" I asked. "Oh, in our living room!" Margarete Holzman showed me a photograph of her family in the same living room, in front of the same bookcase, taken by Herr Löw himself, and she showed me photographs of herself and her sister taken by Rudolf Kaufmann using the Multifoto process.

---

* *Baltic Journey*, a book published by S. Fischer, Frankfurt, in 1994.

The Holzman family in their living room in Kaunas, 1940. On the sofa, Max Holzman and his younger daughter Margarete; at the table, his wife Helene and their elder daughter Marie. Margarete Holzman has a story to tell of that sofa: a nephew of the novelist Lion Feuchtwanger, named Klaus Feuchtwanger, who was also lodging with the Holzmans, kept warning the family that Lithuania would be invaded from either the East or the West, and advised them to emigrate in good time. When Max Holzman bought the new sofa, which could be unfolded and turned into a bed—Rudolf Kaufmann sometimes slept on it—Klaus Feuchtwanger was so exasperated by this ill-timed demonstration of the family's intention to stay put that he refused to exchange a word with his hosts for three days. Max and Marie Holzman were murdered after the German invasion. The photograph was taken by Herr Löw, the "nice man" with whom Rudolf Kaufmann is sitting in the photograph on p. 72, an emigrant from the Soviet Union who also stayed with the Holzman family for some time. Löw, according to Margarete Holzman, was one of about 2000 Jews for whom the Japanese consul in Kaunas obtained visas allowing them to escape from Lithuania and go to Shanghai.

*Rudolf Kaufmann was still experimenting with the Multifoto process in Kaunas,
and the daughters of the bookseller Holzman, Marie (in the white collar) and
Margarete modeled for him. He himself can be seen in the photo top right.*

This fortuitous stroke of luck was followed only a few days later by success in my inquiries. I could have asked the Freiburg city archives long before this for information about the fate of Rudolf Kaufmann's father and his second family. However, I waited until my manuscript was ready and it became a matter of urgency to discover whether, unlikely as it seemed, there might be any heirs or relations of Rudolf Kaufmann whose permission I must ask in order to quote at length from private letters. The surname is too common for anyone to inquire about particular families called Kaufmann in Germany, Great Britain, or America without further clues. I was really only trying to safeguard myself by asking for information in Freiburg. I expected to hear that the family had emigrated, or had been deported and murdered, or that no one knew what had become of them. Instead, I received a copy of a card from the registry office, from which I gathered that the Kaufmanns had survived the war in Freiburg, Walter Kaufmann had died in 1947, and his son by his second marriage, born in 1934, was named Raimund Ludwig. I knew of this son's existence: two of Rudolf Kaufmann's letters to Inge Magnusson mention playing with his little brother on a visit to Freiburg at Easter 1936, but he does not give the child's real first name, only a pet name. I also knew that of all Rudolf Kaufmann's family, this half brother was the most likely to be still alive, but I could hardly go looking for someone called "Hasi." I could, however, look for Raimund Kaufmann. The CD providing information about all telephone subscribers in Germany came up with eight people of that name. The same day that I heard from Freiburg, I sent eight identical letters to eight men of the same name, at eight different addresses in Gelsenkirchen, Menden, Cologne, Trunkelsberg, Hüttlingen,

Düsseldorf, Offenburg, and Hamm. Next day I had two phone calls, one around midday from Trunkelsberg, from a Raimund Kaufmann who told me that his family came from the Swabian Mountains, not Königsberg, and one toward evening from Düsseldorf: "Raimund Kaufmann speaking—I think I'm the man you're looking for."

Naturally, Raimund Kaufmann was amazed by the series of finds and coincidences that had led me to him, but even in that first phone call he dispelled my fears that I might be warned off private property at the last minute as a trespasser. He confirmed what I had suspected from the letters: his parents had thought it necessary to shield him from his elder half brother. Even as an adolescent he had believed that Rudolf was only an uncle. Later, however, the deception itself spurred him on to investigate the family history that had been kept from him so long. Raimund Kaufmann gave me everything he had collected and collated—letters, documents, photographs—so that I could complete my manuscript and tie up the loose ends of the story. He told me about the dead; his eldest half brother Albert, deported from Cologne to Theresienstadt and murdered there; Hans, who died in St Gall in the mid-1960s; Liese, who died in Israel in the early 1950s; Trude, who died in 1995 in the United States. And he told me about the living: Curt Teichert in Washington; Vera, who had married again after her husband's death; and Ilse—Ilse Kaufmann, who had survived the war and emigrated to the United States. Raimund Kaufmann was not sure whether the address he had noted down on a visit fifteen years before would still find her.

I wrote to Ilse Kaufmann, sending her my manuscript and a tape of the radio broadcast. After three weeks, receiving no answer, I phoned her in New York. At eighty-three, she told me, she didn't see at all well and could hardly read, which was why she hadn't replied, but my letter and part of the manuscript had been read aloud to her and she had listened to the tape. She had no objections; indeed, in a way she was glad. I asked her how she managed, living in New York. A nurse came to her little apartment on 72nd Street near Central Park five days a week, she told me. "Opposite Dakota House. Does the name John Lennon mean anything to you? I could hear the shots from my window when he was murdered."

For years she had known nothing of her own husband's death. His Lithuanian colleagues, Ilse Kaufmann told me, had hidden him for a long time, first at the university and then out in the country. He was described simply as "missing" until after the war. Only then did information about the exact circumstances of Rudolf Kaufmann's death emerge.

The news reached me at a late stage too. It came from the living people I had found at last and who showed me that I was by no means, as I had long supposed, the only one to keep Rudolf Kaufmann's memory alive. Margarete Holzman had already mentioned a bicycle borrowed from her mother by Rudolf Kaufmann to go out to a limestone or gypsum quarry near Kaunas. He never came back from that expedition, she said. Among the papers in Raimund Kaufmann's possession there is a letter dated July 1946, written by one Helene Heitmann in Berlin and addressed to Raimund's brother Hans in London:

Dear Herr Kaufmann,

As it happens, I can give you a precise answer to your inquiries about your brother. A woman from Königsberg called Fräulein Jöresch, formerly employed by Consul Jaffa—a personal friend of his too, she worked in Kaunas during the war—did a great deal for the Jews there, particularly the Jews from Königsberg, and I have my information from her. Your brother was protected by the Lithuanians after the German occupation—he worked with them. One day he was out cycling in the country when two German soldiers stopped him. One of them said, that's the Jew Kaufmann from Königsberg, my fiancée, or perhaps he said my wife, was in domestic service in his parents' house, I know him very well. Then they killed him. His wife was in the Vilnius ghetto. She managed to escape—Fräulein Jöresch took her to some farming people near Kaunas, where she had to work hard but she was safe. After Kaunas was evacuated by the Germans— well, I'm afraid I've heard nothing about Fräulein Jöresch or your sister-in-law, but I imagine your sister-in-law is still alive. . . . If she stayed on in K. it will probably be difficult to get in touch with her. By the way, Frau Kaufmann didn't know about her husband's death; Fräulein Jöresch told me she was hoping to be reunited with him. . . .

Rudolf Kaufmann's letters to Ingeborg Magnusson had reached the auction in Frankfurt by accident. Greta Magnusson some-times passes stamps on to a dealer, and one day, not realizing what they contained, she gave him a bundle of envelopes from Germany with rather unusual postmarks.

A postscript for the new edition of 2004 (from which this English version has been translated): The explanation for the appearance of Rudolf Kaufmann's letters in Frankfurt given above turns out to be incorrect. I had been too quick to take as fact this plausible suggestion made by a woman friend of Greta Magnusson, who helped with the exchange of information between us. A few months after the book appeared Greta Magnusson, who had now read the German edition, wrote telling me how it had actually happened:

Stockholm, 26.11.1996

Dear Herr Kaiser,

... one wonders how the letters came to be up for auction? I have thought about it a good deal. It was not my doing. A few days after your last letter I suddenly realized in the middle of the night how it had come about. In 1984 No. 66 [the Skeppargatan building] was being renovated, and I was living in another apartment in the building. Cartons of small items were stored in the cellar. A burglar broke into the cellar in the spring of 1984. That fall the police called me and said that they had found letters with the name and address of Ingeborg M. in the possession of a thief.

However, many of Rudolf Kaufmann's letters to Ingeborg Magnusson did not return to her sister and were lost for the time being. At some time during the next few years they must have crossed the threshold from the underworld to the legitimate world of the stamp trade and stamp collectors. At least, the Frankfurt auctioneer assured me, it was not a thief but an honest Swedish collector of his acquaintance who sent the letters stolen in 1984 to the Frankfurt auction in 1991. "The ways of the Lord are wonderful," Greta Magnusson concludes her letter to me of 1996.

NOTES

p. 4
Mine lilla kaere Ingeborg—postcard, undated. Bologna, June 1935.

p. 8
Tomorrow I'm sending you—Bologna, 27.6.1935.

p. 10
You would be just the right lifelong companion—Bologna, 7.7.1935.

p. 11
We were even officially engaged—ibid.

p. 12
Chiusa con baci—Königsberg, 8.8.1935.

p. 12
Ti ho troppo abbraciato—Königsberg, 20.9.1935.

p. 13
It doesn't matter if they keep—Königsberg, 24.9.1935.

p. 15
. . . then my brother must lend us the collapsible boat—Bologna, 7.7.1935.

p. 15
It's a seaside resort—Georgenswalde, postmarked 30.7.1935.

p. 16
But I realize that my company—Königsberg, 8.8.1935.

p. 16
After 2 long, bitter years—Königsberg, 18.8.1935.

p. 17
However, I don't intend to tell you—Königsberg, 8.8.1935.

p. 17
I feel as if you were sitting here with me—Königsberg, 16.9.1935.

Reinhard Kaiser

p. 21
We poor stupid creatures—Königsberg, 8.8.1935.

p. 22
I hope it will be all right about the visa—Königsberg, 19.9.1935.

p. 22
... one as private assistant to a scientist—Königsberg, 3.10.1935.

p. 23
My dear little signora, *hurrah*—Königsberg, 6.10.1935.

p. 23
I hope I won't forget my shaving kit—Königsberg, 3.10.1935.

p. 24
I have my shaving kit with me!!!—Marienburg, 8.10.1935.

p. 25
A week ago today—Coburg, 10.10.1935.

p. 26
The house stands in a very, very beautiful large park—Coburg, 16.10.1935.

p. 26
Well, I've already settled in here in Coburg—Coburg, 20.10.1935.

p. 28
I'm on the go from morning to night—Coburg, 20.10.1935.

p. 28
... and then we went uphill—Coburg, 11.11.1935.

p. 29
I have to play "Ghosts" with them every evening—ibid.

p. 30
If you could bring some butter and cake from Sweden—Coburg, 9.12.1935.

p. 31
I'm going to Erfurt this afternoon—Coburg, 6.1.1936.

p. 32
I'm starting to learn Hebrew—Coburg, 28.1.1936.

p. 32
Away from the world here—Coburg, 19.2.1936.

p. 34
It's been celebrated—Coburg, 4.3.1936.

p. 35
...invented a dust-shield—Coburg, 22.3.1936.

p. 36
I have such fun with my little brother—Freiburg, 17.4.1936.

p. 36
It's nice for the boys here too—Coburg, 8.5.1936.

p. 37
On Sunday your little husband—Coburg, 17.6.1936.

p. 38
So much has happened—Coburg, 5.6.1936.

p. 39
Would you believe it—Coburg, 9.7.1936.

p. 40
Luckily it's only a few days now—Coburg, 29.7.1936.

p. 42
Arrested for offenses—Bayerische Ostmark, Coburger Nationalzeitung, 1/2. 8.1936,
p. 3.

p. 46
Thank you with all my heart—Coburg, 24.9.1936.

p. 47
Offense Against the Race Laws in Coburg—Der Stürmer, no.4, January 1937, p. 1.

p. 50
Dearest R., I have heard all about it from Trude—undated, Stockholm,
December 1936.

p. 52
Yes, it's really true—Coburg, 10.2.1937.

p. 53
My appeal has been thrown out in Leipzig—Coburg, 22.2.1937.

p. 54
Dear Father . . . I have been given permission to learn English—Amberg, 23.1.1938.

p. 55
It's winter now—Trude Teichert to Ingeborg Magnusson, summer, 1938.

p. 58
You know, harsh as it may sound—Vera Kaufmann to Ingeborg Magnusson,
London, 23.11.1938.

p. 59
And now to another question—Trude Teichert to Ingeborg Magnusson,
1.2.1939.

p. 59
So now I can write to you—Amberg, 26.3.1939.

p. 61
Dear Hans and Vera, dear Inge. Thank you—Amberg, 3.9.1939.

p. 63
Yes, it's not a dream—Cologne, 14.10.1939.

p. 64
. . . chosen by fate—ibid.

Reinhard Kaiser

p. 64
Not at once—ibid.

p. 65
… what all of us in the same situation here do—Düsseldorf, 21.10.1939.

p. 65
… because all the companies want to be rid of us—Düsseldorf, 5.1.1939.

p. 65
And if you don't mind my asking—Düsseldorf, 21.10.1939.

p. 66
You write that you were "nearly unfaithful to me"—Düsseldorf, 5.11.1939.

p. 67
Ingelein, can't you summon up the courage—Düsseldorf, 27.10.1939.

p. 68
It's been suggested to me—Königsberg, 16.11.1939.

p. 69
I have a very adventurous time behind me—Kaunas, 15.1.1940.

p. 70
It's all very well to keep telling myself—Kaunas, 15.4.1940.

p. 70
For the time being we must be glad—Kaunas, 20.3.1940.

p. 70
Every day I realize—Kaunas, 29.3.1940.

p. 71
It's so nice that letters to you—Kaunas, 15.1.1940.

p. 71
I won't say much about Kaunas—Kaunas, 30.12.1939.

p. 73
I hope I can soon go to Vilnius—Kaunas, 20.4.1940.

p. 73
I'm afraid I don't feel really Jewish—Kaunas, 10.3.1940.

p. 74
It seems to us all a miracle—Kaunas, 27.4.1940.

p. 75
All these years of separation—Kaunas, 9.6.1940.

p. 76
Be that as it may—Kaunas, 16.6.1940.

p. 78
I am so sick at heart today—Kaunas, 2.7.1940.

p. 79
It is five-thirty in the afternoon—Pajesia, 22.8.1940.

Notes

p. 80
It's a pity you can't be here with me—Pajesia, 5.9.1940.

p. 81
. . . one a little reproachful—Skirsnemune, 11.3.1941.

BIBLIOGRAPHY

Deutschland-Berichte der Sozialdemokratischen Partei Deutschlands (Sopade), vol. 3. Reprint. Salzhausen: Verlag Petra Nettelbeck; Frankfurt: Zweitausendeins, 1980. (1936), p. 1663.

Verena Dohrn. *Baltische Reise. Vielvölkerlandschaft des alten Europa.* Frankfurt: S. Fischer, 1994, p. 182.

Hubert Fromm. *Die Coburger Juden. Geschichte und Schicksal.* Coburg: Druckhaus Neue Presse 1990, pp. 88, 207 ff., 219.

Antoni Hoffman, Wolf-Ernst Reif. Rudolf Kaufmann's work on iterative evolution in the Upper Cambrian trilobite genus *Olenus*: a reappraisal. In: *Paläontologische Zeitschrift* 68, 1/2, pp. 71–87. Stuttgart: Schweizerbart'sche Verlagsbuchhandlung, March 1994.

List of Displaced German Scholars. London, autumn 1936, ed. the Notgemeinschaft deutscher Wissenschaftler im Ausland. In: *Emigration, Deutsche Wissenschaftler nach 1933. Entlassung und Vertreibung.* Berlin: Technische Universität, 1987, p. 40.

Horst R. Sassin. *Widerstand, Verfolgung und Emigration Liberaler, 1933–1944*, ed. the Frierich Nauman Stiftung. Bonn: Liberal Verlag, 1983, p. 29f.

Curt Teichert. Obituary. Rudolf Kaufmann. *American Journal of Science* 1946, 244, pp. 808–810.

PICTURE REFERENCES

Pp. 4, 6, 13, 49, 72, 89, 91: from the author's archive. Pp. 7, 14, 24: by kind permission of Greta Magnusson, Stockholm. P. 9: trilobite specimens from Rudolf Kaufmann's dissertation, *Variationstatistische Untersuchungen über die "Artabwandlung" und "Artumbildung" an der Oberkambrischen Trilobitengattung Olenus Dalm*," Greisfswald 1933 (p. 35). Pp. 19, 42, 47, 48: by kind permission of Raimund Kaufmann, Düsseldorf. P. 26: The Pupils of the Preacher Hirsch boarding school, from Hubert Fromm, *Die Coburger Juden. Geschichte und Schicksal.* Coburg 1990. Pp. 94, 95: by kind permission of Margarete Holzman, Giessen.

ACKNOWLEDGMENTS

I would like to thank Greta Magnusson in Stockholm for her generosity in sending me the letters written by Rudolf Kaufmann to her sister that were still in her hands, and some photographs; Klaus-Jürgen Liedtke in Berlin for his help with the writing of an important letter; Marianne Friedländer in Berlin for her kind information; H.-J. Baier, Dip. Arch. in Coburg, for his expertise in guiding me to important documents; Margarete Holzman in Giessen for family photos and Multifotos, and an afternoon full of stories and reminiscences; Prof. Raimund Kaufmann in Düsseldorf for advice and help, and his generosity in making available to me all the material he had collected about his half brother; my mother, Ruth Kaiser in Viersen, for preparing the photographs reproduced in this book; and Ilse Kaufmann in New York for the goodwill she showed to my project when at last she heard of it, and for permission to quote as extensively from her husband's letters as I have done.

I would also like to thank all who listened to me during my researches and my attempt to write this boook, gave me their

Reinhard Kaiser

time, and encouraged me by their attention, in particular my
wife Viktoria, my daughter Lisa, and my son Matthis, as well as
Hans-Peter Kensy, Gerd Ellenbeck, Klaus Crummenerl, Franziska
Altenpohl, Alexander von Plato, Leonie Wannenmacher, and
the classes of the grammar schools in the Märkischer Kreis district, to whom I introduced this story in its early version in
1995, and whose interest, more than anything else, prevented me
from postponing the task of turning the radio version into a book.

Finally, I would like to thank the Märkische Kulturkonferenz,
whose literary stipend for the year 1995 was a considerable help
to me in my work on this book.

R.K.
Frankfurt am Main, 20 February 1996